W9-BNS-176

THE
ROAD
TO
ARMAGEDDON

CHARLES R.
SWINDOLL

JOHN F.
WALVOORD

J. DWIGHT
PENTECOST

AND OTHER MEMBERS OF THE DALLAS SEMINARY FACULTY

WORD PUBLISHING
NASHVILLE
A Thomas Nelson Company

Library of Congress Cataloging-in-Publication Data

Swindoll, Charles R.
The road to armageddon : a biblical understanding of prophecy and end time
events / Charles R. Swindoll, John F. Walvoord, J. Dwight Pentecost, and
members of the Dallas Theological Seminary Faculty.
p.   cm.

ISBN 0-8499-1619-4

1. Bible—Prophecies—End of the world—Sermons.   2. End of the world—
Biblical teaching—Sermons.   3. Evangelical Free Church of America—Sermons.
4. Sermons, American.   I. Walvoord, John F.   II. Pentecost, J. Dwight.   III. Title.

BS649.E63S85   1999   98-55911
236'.9—dc21   CIP

Printed in the United States of America
99 00 01 02 03 04 05 06   BVG   9 8 7 6 5 4 3 2

CONTENTS

DR. CHARLES R. SWINDOLL

Practical Advice for Perilous Times

CHARLES R.
SWINDOLL

President, Dallas Theological Seminary

D R. CHARLES R. SWINDOLL is president of Dallas Theological Seminary and host of the internationally syndicated radio program, "Insight for Living." He is also the senior pastor of Stonebridge Community Church in Frisco, Texas. He has authored more than twenty-five best-selling books, including *Esther, David, The Grace Awakening,* and *Laugh Again.* His practical application of the Bible to everyday living makes God's truths a reality to hurting people. Dr. Swindoll and his wife Cynthia reside in Dallas, Texas.

CHAPTER
ONE

Practical Advice for Perilous Times

Before I was a student at Dallas Seminary, my dad felt that I should learn a trade. So I worked as a machinist's apprentice for four and a half years, serving a trade in which I would later become a journeyman machinist while working my way through school.

During that period of time I got to know a number of interesting people and developed an appreciation for those who earn a living with their hands. That whole blue-collar world is familiar to me, and to this day I recall some wonderful folks I got to know in the shop. One of them was a guy we'll call Tex. This was in Houston, and Tex and I worked second shift along with about three hundred other fellows in a large machine shop. Tex was one of those characters you think of when you think of a machinist. He wore overalls that he changed the oil in about once a month. He had a bandana that hung out of his hip pocket. Every day he wore the same gray-and-white, greasy cap pulled down almost to his ears. I think he changed the oil in the cap about every two years. Same cap, same overalls, same bandana, and in the other hip pocket he had a big pouch of chewing tobacco.

> ### *"I stay ready to keep from getting ready."*

He and I worked on the turret lathes. I worked just behind Tex and would watch him through those hot Houston evenings. He was as predictable as he could be. About thirty minutes after supper, he would reach into his pouch of chewing tobacco. All through the evening, he'd chew that tobacco and he'd spit.

STAY READY TO KEEP FROM GETTING READY

Tex was one of these guys who have unique little phrases about life. People who work in shops like that often sort of boil life down into simple statements. You need to understand, if you've never worked in a shop, that your life is controlled by a whistle. A whistle tells you when work starts. A whistle tells you when it's time for lunch, or for dinner, and a whistle tells you when it's time to go home. It's called "quittin' time." Tex never wore a watch, but he had this inner sensor that let him know the time without even checking. He always knew what time it was, and he would say to me on occasion, "Well, it's about time for supper, Sonny." He always called me Sonny. Sure enough, within a minute or two that whistle would blow. And I always noticed that Tex was ready to go home before anybody else. In fact I said to him one night, "Well, you about ready for quittin' time?" He said, "Sonny, let me tell you something. I stay ready to keep from gettin' ready. I stay ready for quittin' time." Years passed before I thought about that phrase again. One day while I was in a class at Dallas Seminary studying the events of the future, I recall one of the profs saying he supposed we could call these future things "when it's quitting time on earth." And I suddenly remembered Tex's words. "I stay ready to keep from gettin' ready."

In a mixed group of people, I realize there are all kinds of responses to future things, prophecy, and prophetic events. Some of you probably think it's somewhere between a joke and a leap into a dark room. You're not convinced of any of this, and you're probably reading this out of idle curiosity wondering what all this prophetic interest is about. Maybe you were attracted by the title, *The Road to Armageddon and Beyond.* You might, in the back of your mind, be thinking, "I'm not convinced." In fact when you hear words like, "The Lord Himself will descend from heaven with a shout, with the voice of the archangel and with the trumpet of God, and the dead in Christ shall rise first" (1 Thess. 4:16), you might think, "Wait a minute. You've already left me. A voice, a shout, a trumpet?" At Dallas Seminary our chaplain, Bill Bryant, plays the trumpet. I often have a lot of fun with Bill as he says the only instrument that's going to be used in heaven is the trumpet. So I found a cute little piece the other day that some wag wrote: "Due to the shortage of trained trumpeters, the end of the world will be postponed three months!"

While some folks choose to laugh about end times, other people aren't laughing. We recently received a letter from a man who's not laughing, or didn't for a long time, even though I'm sure he passed off things about the future as sort of a joke or something to laugh about. He wrote:

> By the time I had reached my mid-twenties, I was ready to die. I was drinking heavily and participating in all the immoral acts that usually accompany a drunken, selfish, godless lifestyle. Ironically, I had it all. Had a great job, drove a new car, I had, I had, I had, but I truly had nothing. I can't count the number of times during that era that I placed the barrel of a cocked and fully loaded .357 in my mouth, or against my head and thought how simple it would be to end it all. That's how it was and that is how it seemed it would always be to me.

Some of you live in a world like that, and when you think about the future you think, "It's kind of a pie in the sky by and by that'll meet the needs for some folks, but not me." And then there are those who sort of yawn and think, "I'll kind of lean back and listen because I'm somewhat interested in these kinds of things, but it's really a matter of curiosity for me. I'm not all that concerned about now, and, far as I know, when we die, we'll die like dogs and there won't be any tomorrow."

No one put it better than Billy Graham in his great book *World Aflame* as he described the complacency of our times.

> In a declining culture, one of its characteristics is that ordinary people are unaware of what is happening. Only those who know and can read the signs of decadence are posing the questions that as yet have no answer. Mr. Average Man is comfortable in his complacency and is

unconcerned as a silverfish in a carton of discarded magazines on world affairs. He is not asking any questions because his social benefits from the government give him a false sense of security. This is his trouble and his tragedy. Modern man has become a spectator of world events, observing on his television screen without becoming involved. He watches the ominous events of our times pass before his eyes while he sips his beer in a comfortable chair. He does not seem to realize what is happening to him. He does not understand that his world is on fire, and he is about to be burned up with it.[1]

And then there are those like Tex who can say, "I don't have to get ready. I stay ready." For those of you in that category, the coming of the Lord Jesus represents a sure promise yet to be fulfilled, the anticipated hope that you live your life for—that final dramatic scene when God breaks through the sky and sends His Son, as Dr. Walvoord will discuss in the next chapter. "And we meet Him in the clouds in the air, and so shall we ever be with the Lord" (1 Thess. 4:17 KJV).

LIVING IN PERILOUS TIMES

But that's then, and this is now. What about today? What about now? A. W. Tozer put it in an interesting way. "We think of ourselves as inhabiting some parenthetic interval between the God who was and the God who will be, and in this ever present now, we are lonely with that ancient and cosmic loneliness." What about now in the loneliness of today?

As Francis Schaeffer asked, "How shall we then live?" I want

5

to build a case for how bad things are today, and why we need the promise of a change. Second Timothy 3:1 states, "Realize this, that in the last days, difficult times will come." Perilous times. Hard times. The word translated "difficult" means "hard to bear, violent, vicious, savage." Its only other use in the New Testament is in Matthew 8:28, where Matthew describes two men who had demons and were out of control. They were wild like an untamed animal. Like a storm that's out of control. That's the word used in Second Timothy for difficult: hard to bear, storm-tossed. One of my mentors used to refer to this as savage. We're living in savage times. It's not that they will come, it's that they *have* come.

Think for a moment over the last six, eight, ten months of evening news on the television. Bad times? Hard times? Perilous times? Remember when the playground used to be where kids played? Now it's a battleground. One of my grandchildren not yet in junior high school told me when we visited his family in California recently, "They've decided that we have to walk through metal detectors now to come to school." He's in sixth grade, going through metal detectors. Remember when we used to play barefoot outside? I remember playing "kick the can" until it was dark. Kicking the can messed my toes up because we were barefooted, but we had a lot of fun. We were playing cops and robbers and nobody even thought anybody would be hurt. No longer. The family is in perilous times.

Stephen Covey, in his book, *The Seven Habits of Highly Effective Families*, breaks our heart with these facts.

> Over the past thirty years, the situation for families has changed powerfully and dramatically. Illegitimate birth

6

rates have increased more than 400 percent. The percentage of families headed by a single parent has more than tripled. The divorce rate has more than doubled. Teenage suicide has increased almost 300 percent. Scholastic Aptitude Test scores among all students have dropped seventy-three points. The number one health problem for American women today is domestic violence. One fourth of all adolescents contract a sexually transmitted disease before they graduate from high school.[2]

Do you know what the problems were in 1940 in the classrooms of the schools? Covey mentions them. Talking out of turn, chewing gum, making noise, running in the halls, cutting in line, dress code infractions, and littering. You know what the problems are in the schools in the 1990s?

> **Things are not turning out well, they are turning out wrong.**

Drug abuse, alcohol abuse, pregnancy, suicide, rape, robbery, and assault.

HOPE IS NEEDED

Men and women, perilous times have come. We are not getting better and better. Things are not turning out well, they are turning out wrong. That means we need some hope. We need to know there's a change on the horizon. We also need to know that the Bible addresses how we live in times like these. Generally speaking, there are words that appear all the way through the Gospels. For example, go to Matthew 24. Let me show you some general statements made by our Savior, the Lord Jesus Christ.

If you like marking your Bibles, you may find it interesting to mark repeated statements that are commands to us. Matthew 24:42, "Therefore be on the alert for you do not know which day your Lord is coming." Verse 44 states: "For this reason, you be ready for the Son of Man is coming at an hour when you do not think He will." Be on the alert. You be ready.

Look at Mark 13:21–23, "And then if anyone says to you, 'Behold, here is the Christ'; or, 'Behold, He is there'; do not believe him; for false Christs and false prophets will arise, and will show signs and wonders, in order, if possible, to lead the elect astray. But take heed;" From Matthew we read be on the alert. You be ready. Now from Mark, "Take heed; behold I have told you everything in advance." Continue on with verse 33: "Take heed, keep on the alert for you do not know when the appointed time is." Verse 35: "Therefore, be on the alert for you do not know when the master of the house is coming." Verse 37: "And what I say to you I say to all, 'Be on the alert. Again and again and again, be ready, be on the alert, stay ready, keep ready.

Now go to Luke 21:34–36, "Be on guard that your hearts may not be weighted down with dissipation and drunkenness and the worries of life, and that day come on you suddenly like a trap; for it will come upon all those who dwell on the face of all the earth. But keep on the alert at all times, praying in order that you may have strength to escape."

Look at John 14. I love this section of Scripture. Jesus ministers to His twelve. They have followed Him, eaten alongside Him, slept beside Him, watched Him do His work, been mentored by Him, and shared their lives with Him. Now they come to the end in this small upper room, and He unveils to them a plan they were not ready to hear. Verse 1: "Let not your heart be troubled; believe in God, believe also in Me." And then He turns to the future. He tells them not to be troubled about today. Look to the future. "In my Father's house are many dwelling places; if it were not so, I would have told you; for I go to prepare a place for you. And if I go and prepare a place for you, I will come again, and receive you to Myself; that where I am, there you may be also."

> **God is not hesitant to reveal the truth of the future as He predicts and commands us to be ready for what is coming.**

MARCHING ORDERS

It's very surprising to many people that no less than three hundred times in the New Testament alone, future events are mentioned. Three hundred times! And in fact, we know more in the Scriptures about hell than about heaven. God is not hesitant to reveal the truth of the future as He predicts and commands us to be ready for what is coming. Now in light of that, return to 2 Timothy 3 for some practical advice for perilous times like these.

What are the marching orders for people who live in these perilous, savage, difficult times when the courts are out of control, when the schools are out of control, when neighborhoods are out of control, when it seems as though even your home at times is living on the ragged edge? Let me give you four statements that come from the Scriptures we're looking at toward the end of chapter 3 and the early part of chapter 4. How do we stay ready until quittin' time?

1. *Follow the model of the faithful.* "But you followed my teaching, conduct, purpose, faith, patience, love, perseverance, persecution, sufferings such as happened to me at Antioch, at Iconium, and at Lystra; what persecutions I endured, and out of them all the Lord delivered me! And indeed, all those who desire to live godly in Christ Jesus will be persecuted" (2 Tim. 3:10–12).

You see how Paul put it? You, Timothy, have followed my model. What does it mean to follow the model of the faithful? It means we watch their lives. It means we learn from their example. It means we listen to their instruction. We emulate their virtues. We admire their character. We remember what they endured, and in light of that it helps our endurance. There's something wonderful about having faithful mentors and faithful heroes in the annuls of history.

Hebrews 11 is full of those names, and toward the end of that chapter the writer says, "What shall I more say? for the time would fail me to tell of," and then he names them, "Gideon, and of Barak, and of Samson, and Jephthah; and of David also, and Samuel, and of the prophets: who through faith subdued kingdoms, wrought righteousness, obtained promises, stopped the mouths of lions, quenched the violence of fire, escaped the edge of the sword, out of weakness were made strong, waxed valiant in fight, turned to flight the armies of the aliens. . . . And others were tortured, . . . sawn asunder. . . . They wandered about in sheepskins and goatskins; being destitute, afflicted, tormented; (of whom the world was not worthy)" (Heb. 11:32–38 KJV).

Do not believe that because our times are hard there are not people worth following and there are not models worth emulating. There's something inspiring about knowing that someone has gone ahead of us and walked the walk, and lived the life. In light of their example we can do the same.

I thought about that recently when I came across a story about a five-hundred-mile dogsled race over a part of Minnesota in the mid-winter months. You may have read about Susan Butcher, who won that race two years in a row. We're talking pioneer woman. She pressed on through bitter cold and howling winds of a blizzard, dark nights and exhausting days, as her well-trained huskies pulled her sled over those hundreds of miles from the start to the finish of the race. At the end of the race, she was interviewed and was asked, "How in the world did you stay at it?" You know her answer. "I just remembered that others have done it before me, and I could do it too. Because they did it, so can I." It's unbelievable what she endured. Ten to twelve days in the middle of nowhere, maddening monotony, strained beyond belief. How did she do it? She did it like composers who stay at the music until they get it composed. She did it like people who write books and stay at it until they get all the chapters completed. She did it like mothers of the young stay at it until they get their children reared and out of the house. She is like all the rest of us. She followed the model of those who have gone before her. And so can you. And so must I.

> Do not believe that because our times are hard there are not people worth following and there are not models worth emulating.

Men and women, when you get weary of the perilous times,

call to mind one of your heroes, one of your mentors. Remember there are those who have faithfully lived before you and made it, and you can too. Follow the model of the faithful.

2. *Stay with the truth of the Bible.* "But evil men and imposters will proceed from bad to worse, deceiving and being deceived. You, however, [similar to the "but you" at the beginning of verse 10] "continue in the things you have learned and become convinced of, knowing from whom you have learned them;"—and then Paul gets a very tender thought—"and that from childhood you have known the sacred writings which are able to give you the wisdom that leads to salvation through faith which is in Christ Jesus" (2 Tim. 3:13–15).

> **If you stay with the truth of the Bible, you'll never go wrong.**

If you stay with the truth of the Bible, you'll never go wrong. It will never discourage you and it will never lead you astray. My first thought was to say this point ought to read, "Stay with the teaching of your past," and then I remembered not everyone has been as blessed as I have been, and as many of us have been.

My mind goes back to a little home on Quince Street in East Houston where I was raised. My mother, who loved the Lord dearly, used to challenge us as children to memorize verses of Scripture. She would memorize two verses for every one we would memorize, and when I got into junior high school I thought, "I'm going to show her. I'm going to out-memorize her. I'm going to drive her under the table." So I memorized the book of James. She memorized the book of Hebrews. I decided, "I'm not going there."

Maybe that wasn't your background. Maybe that wasn't the

way you were trained or brought up. If not, it's regrettable, because there's something about following, staying with the teachings of the past. But if that doesn't fit you, how about staying with the truths of the Scriptures? Maybe you didn't have the parents you wish you had. Maybe you don't have a background that you can draw on in days like this. Listen, you've got the Scriptures. Look at Timothy's case, verse 15: "From childhood you have known the sacred writings." From childhood. How could that be? I'm glad you asked. Look at chapter 1, verse 5, of Second Timothy. Paul again remembers Timothy's past, and he says, "I am mindful of the sincere faith within you, which first dwelt in your grandmother Lois, and in your mother Eunice. And I am sure it is in you as well." Timothy had great roots. Paul thinks back to Timothy's grandmother Lois and his mother Eunice. Both of them on his maternal side poured themselves into young Timothy as he was growing up. He learned the ways of God from those in his family.

Go back to 2 Timothy 3:15. Please observe the substance of Timothy's training: "The sacred writings which are able to give you the wisdom that leads to salvation through faith which is in Christ Jesus." Take time to dwell on that. *In these perilous days take time for that Bible class, take time for personal study, take the time to dwell in the Word of God.*

If you didn't have a mother or a grandmother like Timothy had, you can still become like those wise women. I was helping Peninsula Bible Church celebrate its fiftieth anniversary recently. It was a wonderful time of nostalgia. As memories flowed over me. I was blessed to have known Ray Stedman personally as one of his early interns along with Luis Palau. Luis came with his wife Pat and their twin babies in 1961, the same year I was there. Luis, Gib Martin, and I poured our lives into that church, and the church into ours. It was wonderful to go back and to celebrate fifty years of history, and it occurred to me how valuable are roots like that and people like Ray Stedman in my life.

While I was there, I was in the home of longtime friends, one of whom is a new grandmother named Sue. She couldn't let go of her little grandbaby. She just held her the whole time she was eating. While she was loving on this little grandbaby and enjoying her, she said, "You know what, Chuck? My role now has changed. I realize now that I am to pour my life into these little ones that my children bring into the world." Isn't that a great perspective?

So I speak to you who are grandparents and great-grandparents. There's something wonderful about passing along the truths of God's Word to those little ones who believe you when you're a grandparent. They just believe you. It's so wonderful you don't have to earn their trust. (Why didn't we have them first? Wouldn't that have been easier?) They just sit and blink their eyes and listen and drink it in. Pour it into them. They're like little birds with their mouths open. And what is it we pour into them? Salvation through faith which is in Christ Jesus. All Scripture inspired by God, profitable for teaching, for reproof, for correction, for training in righteousness. Teaching the truth, refuting error, cultivation of manners in life, and the disciplines in right living. That's what we get from the Scriptures.

In a world where everything has turned gray and become a blur, the Scriptures still mark the lines between right and wrong, between good and evil, between blessed and cursed. Teach your children and grandchildren the Scriptures. Stay with the teachings of the Scriptures.

3. *Proclaim the message of Christ.* "I solemnly charge you in the presence of God and of Christ Jesus, who is to judge the living and the dead,"—there's another future statement, another subject we'll be getting into in our prophetic conference, judging the living and the dead—"and by His appearing and His kingdom"—that's another statement regarding the future, all part of future teaching, all part of God's prophetic plan—"preach the word" (2 Tim. 4:12). Proclaim, herald the message. As we move into the fourth chapter of Second Timothy, we get a little more insight on how to handle perilous times like these.

Follow the model of the faithful. Stay with the truth of the Bible. Proclaim the message of Christ. In an era like this there is no other message like it. Preach the Word. Be ready. Be consistent. Be faithful in season and out of season. Reprove, rebuke, exhort, but don't be caustic about it. Don't think you can drive it down people's throats. Paul says to do that with great patience and for the purpose of instruction. Proclaim the message of Christ. Press it home, make it clear, say it straight, stand strong. There's a sense of urgency in these words. For you who are not familiar with the motto of Dallas Seminary, we read it in chapter 4 of Second Timothy, verse 2, the first three words. Our motto for these seventy-five years has remained "Preach the Word." When I walk into Chafer Chapel day after day, I usually turn and look at the wall behind me. There stands the seal of the school. It's a hand holding a torch held high. And around the seal, around this symbol of the torch, are the words written from the Greek text, "Preach the Word." It's a reminder to me on a regular basis that our job is to train men and women to proclaim the message of Christ.

Let me give you a little tip. Individually, you go where none of the rest of us ever go. You touch lives that the person sitting behind you, next to you, or even the one married to you will not touch. You're the one, therefore, who must proclaim the message to your sphere of influence. Paul says to do it in season and out of season. I take that literally. Do it when it's convenient, do it when it's not. Do it when you feel like it, do it when you don't feel like it. Do it in the winter, and do it in the summer. Proclaim it when it's appreciated, and proclaim it when it's resented. Do it when others are open, and do it when others are closed. Whether they are young or old, whether it's early or late, whether it's public or private. When you're asked, and when you're not asked. This is not a Biblical mandate for rudeness, for Paul

> You're the one who must proclaim the message to your sphere of influence.

says to do it with patience and to do it for the purpose of instructing (v. 2).

And may I add just a thought here? Keep it simple, very simple. People in perilous times are confused. It's easy for us to dump the truck rather than just give them a little bit to chew on along with our business card that says this is where you can reach me if you have any more questions about these things we've been talking about. Keep it simple.

One of the many stories that has survived the Civil War has to do with a letter that took only three lines from the president's pen. And yet it was the simple message that changed the course of history and ended the war. It was written by President Lincoln, a man known for plain and simple speech, dated April 7, 1865, 11:00 A.M. It was addressed to General Grant. It read: "General Sheridan says, 'If the thing is pressed, I think that Lee will surrender.' Let the thing be pressed." Signed, A. Lincoln. By the ninth day of that same month, two days later, Robert E. Lee surrendered at Appomattox Courthouse. The "thing" was pressed.

In these perilous times when there are all kinds of messages and a cacophony of sounds and an assortment of entertainment, all kinds of things attracting our attention, there is something about the simple declaration of the Gospel that cuts through all the gobbledy-gook and feeds the hungry heart. Follow the model of the faithful. Stay with the truth of the Bible. Proclaim the message of Christ.

4. *Maintain an exemplary life.* "For the time will come when they will not endure sound doctrine;" [May I for a moment change the words "will come" to "have come" or "has come"? 'For the time *has come* when they will not endure sound doctrine'], "but wanting to have their ears tickled, they will accumulate for themselves teachers in accordance to their own desires; and will turn away their ears from the truth, and will turn aside to myths. But you," [sound familiar? see 2 Timothy 3:10, 14; 4:5] "be sober in all things, endure hardship, do the work of an evangelist, fulfill your ministry." All the way through this passage Paul is pushing his finger against Timothy's sternum. "You, Timothy. You listen to me, Timothy, listen to me. This is for you." This can be said to you also. "You, however, maintain an exemplary life." There's your fourth marching order.

People can argue with your philosophy, they can deny your theology, they can bring up all kinds of arguments, all kinds of statements that will get you sidetracked, but there's one thing they can never deny and that's an exemplary life. There is something about a life lived for the glory of God on a campus that the campus will not and cannot ignore. There's something about an exemplary life lived in the office that the people in the office cannot and will not overlook. Maintain an exemplary life. Even though the time has come when people will not endure sound doctrine, Paul says for you to be sober, endure hardship, do the work of an evangelist, fill to the full your ministry. And by the way, we all are engaged in the ministry.

> There's something about an exemplary life that the people cannot and will not overlook.

One man put it this way: "When men and women get intoxicated with heady heresies and sparkling novelties, we must keep calm and sane." Good advice. A calm, sane, exemplary life.

HOW CAN I STAY READY?

Now, how can I keep this up? How can I make this happen on a regular basis? When the prophecy conference ends, when the next year turns, when the next century dawns, when I get older and the Lord has not yet returned, what are the timeless facts that I can count on that will help me maintain this sense of readiness? How can I stay ready to keep from getting ready? In each of the last three verses I want you to see there's a principle worth remembering. Look at verse 6, "I'm already being poured out as drink offering, and the time of my departure has come."

Principle number one. *Consider your life an offering to God rather than a monument to humanity.* The apostle says in the dungeon, "I am already being offered as a drink offering," my head is already on the block. It wasn't long before there was the swish of the blade and Paul's head fell from his shoulders. It wasn't long after this ink had dried that the apostle was taken. His life was an offering to God, not a monument to man.

> Consider your life an offering to God rather than a monument to humanity.

In verse 7, Paul declares: "I have fought the good fight, I have finished the course, I have kept the faith."

Principle number two. *Remember that finishing well is the final proof that truth works.*

Ours is a time of epidemic falling. Falling from the things of Christ. Falling from the privilege of ministry. Let's commit ourselves in this hour to being those who finish well. It's great to meet those who are finishing well; it's wonderful. "I've fought the good fight, I've finished the course, I've kept the faith." That's the final proof that truth works.

Paul confidently states in verse 8: "In the future there is laid up for me the crown of righteousness, which the Lord, the righteous Judge, will award to me on that day; and not only me, but also to all who have loved His appearing." Another reference to the future. And we will hear more about His appearing as our conference continues.

Principle number three. *Fix your eyes on your heavenly reward instead of earthly allurements.* I'm especially fond of the works of C.S. Lewis, as many of you are. I came across a fine statement from his pen that I had not heard before. "It is the second coming of Christ that is the medicine our condition especially needs," writes Lewis. "We must never speak to simple,

19

excitable people about the day [the day Christ comes] without emphasizing again and again our current situation. The great thing is to be found at one's post as a child of God, living each day as though it were our last, but planning as though our world might last a hundred years."

Fix your eyes on your heavenly reward instead of your earthly allurements.

Do you get that? "Living each day as if it were our last, but planning as though our world might last a hundred years." When we do that, we don't have to get ready. We stay ready.

I'd like you to bow your heads, please. I'd like you to close your eyes for just a few moments, just where you are. Imagine in your mind the fulfillment of these words. "The Lord Himself will descend from heaven with a shout, with the voice of the archangel, and with the trumpet of God; and the dead in Christ shall rise first. Then we who are alive and remain, shall be caught up together with them in the clouds to meet the Lord in the air, and thus we shall always be with the Lord. Therefore, comfort one another with these words" (1 Thess. 4:16–18).

If that were to happen this night, this very night, would you be ready? Are you absolutely certain that there has been a time in your life when you have said, "I receive the Lord Jesus Christ as my Savior; I take the gift God has offered; I believe He died for my sins; I believe He rose from the dead, bodily, miraculously, and He lives today for me, bringing all into His family who will receive Him as Savior"? If you've never done that, this is the perfect opportunity for you to prepare for what is indeed to come and may come before we awaken in the morning.

Our Father, I ask that you would honor your Word and you would give us a fresh zeal for living its truths in this world that has lost its way. And rather than condemning our sur-roundings, may we be those who bring hope and light and relief to those who are confused and walk in darkness. Be pleased to bless your Word and the hope it provides. In Jesus' name I ask this. Amen.

DR. JOHN F. WALVOORD

The Rapture: The Next Event on God's Calendar

JOHN F. WALVOORD

Chancellor, Dallas Theological Seminary

D R. JOHN F. WALVOORD is recognized as one of the leading conservative evangelical theologians in America and is Chancellor of Dallas Theological Seminary, where he has served since 1935. An expert in biblical eschatology, he has written or edited thirty-two related books, including *The Rapture Question, The Millennial Kingdom,* and *The Prophecy Knowledge Handbook,* and is a regular contributor to the seminary's theological journal, *Bibliotheca Sacra.* Walvoord and his wife Geraldine reside in Dallas.

CHAPTER
TWO

The Rapture: The Next Event on God's Calendar

This title, *The Road to Armageddon,* is of course, a word of warning to the non-Christian world that they're on a road to disaster, the broad road that leads to destruction as Christ spoke of it (Matt. 7:13).

Now this isn't our main objective in this book, but I think we have to realize that we have alternatives. And one of the alternatives was named by Christ Himself, when He said there was a way of escape though few find it. Now most of you, I think, are aware of the fact that our

When we put our trust in Him, we transfer from the Road to Armageddon to the Road to Glory.

way of escape is through faith in Jesus Christ our Savior, the Son of God, who died on the cross for our sins and rose again.

When we put our trust in Him, we transfer from the Road to Armageddon to the Road to Glory. I don't think it's been given sufficient attention, though it's been discussed in our modern world, that there are consequences for what we do.

God does not force anybody to believe. There are consequences for faith, and there are consequences for unbelief, and it's our duty as Christians to warn people that there is a choice.

Our main purpose here is to describe the Road to Glory and the wonderful fact that Christ is going to come one of these days, perhaps very soon, and take His church out of the world and to heaven before the Road to Armageddon comes to its finale and the world is judged for its sin and unbelief. And that, of course, is what we're discussing here.

Now the approach to the prophecies of the Bible, particularly the rapture of the church which is our present discussion, is a very important doctrine, but we have to face the fact that the world does not believe in prophecy. It's rather interesting to me as a prophecy teacher that whenever there's a crisis, the world suddenly becomes aware of the fact that there are prophecies in the Bible. They may not agree with them, but there's always that sneaking suspicion that possibly we're right, and that they're on the wrong road.

It is also interesting to me, and somewhat surprising, that when the Gulf War broke out practically all the important newspapers of our country had whole pages on the subject of Is This Armageddon? Is this the end of the world? Is this the Second Coming of Christ?" They didn't believe it, but they were entertaining the possibility. Now, of course, the answer was no, the war in Kuwait was not Armageddon. Armageddon is a name given to the final struggle between God and wicked men just before the Second Coming. Armageddon is a place in northern Israel, and the final war will be fought in Israel by millions of men locked in struggle right up to the day of the Second Coming of Christ. Zechariah 14 tells us there will be house-to-house fighting on that very day before the glory of Christ appears in heaven and the armies of the world forget their differences, all to unite against God. But it's all so futile. The Bible says that Christ just speaks the word, the sword out of His mouth, and all these millions of men with their beasts are instantly killed, the most awful judgment of which the Bible has spoken up to that time.

TRUSTING BIBLICAL PROPHECY

How do we know that when we read a prophecy in the Bible it's true? We've already had some statistics on this. I had occasion to examine this question in detail when I wrote my book *Prophecy Knowledge Handbook.* I attempted to do something that I find that no one else has attempted to do, and that is to explain every prophecy in the Bible from Genesis to Revelation. That is a tall order, and I worked it

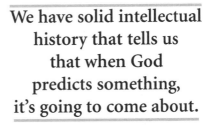

We have solid intellectual history that tells us that when God predicts something, it's going to come about.

through in a year and a half, but, of course, I'd studied the subject before. I knew something about it. I covered about one thousand prophetic passages, some of them single verses, some of them whole chapters, large subjects. When I got through I learned something I hadn't realized before: Half of these prophecies, five hundred passages, had already been literally fulfilled. I wonder about the mathematical possibilities of that. I think it gets up into the trillions, at least.

However, we are not emotionally guided by that conclusion. We have solid intellectual history that tells us that when God predicts something, it's going to come about. This is particularly true about Jesus Christ. Micah had said six hundred years before Christ came into the world that He would be born in Bethlehem. He was born in Bethlehem, not Babylon. Scriptures said He would be a great prophet, and He was a great prophet. That's what Moses described Him as. He was a miracle worker. He healed the sick and the injured and so on as the Old Testament predicted, and He ministered among men. Then, according to Old Testament passages like Isaiah 53 and Psalm 22, He was to die.

How could God become a man and then die? But He did, and His death was with a purpose. He was the perfect Son of God, and He died because He was bearing the sins of the whole world on His shoulders. Somehow His death, though we cannot completely explain it, was God's way of atoning and paying the price for the sins of the whole world. His death on the cross and His resurrection that followed made possible our redemption, not because we deserve it, or attain it, or accomplish something in this life. Only by the grace of God will a person go to heaven, not because he's done something good. In fact, none of us has done everything right, so it's necessary to be saved by grace. And one of the most dramatic fulfilled prophecies in the world was the occasion when Christ died and rose again.

Now that fact leads to God's plan for us—the different road, the different destiny that comes when a person puts his trust in Jesus Christ. In the Old Testament, there were predictions of the first and second coming of Christ, as a word of warning, but nobody understood it, even the writers of Scripture. The common trend was to sort of ignore the sufferings of Christ, and to seize the fact that He was going to come as a glorious ruler. That's what the disciples were expecting; that's why they followed Him. After all, He told them they'd sit on thrones judging the twelve tribes of Israel, but they didn't know that referred to His Second Coming and not His first coming. And so they were misled.

As they followed Christ for three and a half years while nothing happened, it seemed, to go towards that goal, they began to wonder. Judas Iscariot bailed out, of course, and accepted thirty pieces of silver to betray Christ, and four of the other disciples—Peter, Andrew, James, and John—came to Christ privately and said, "Tell us, what is the sign of your coming and the end of the age?" They also asked about His prediction that Jerusalem would be destroyed. None of that fit their theology, that He was going to bring in a glorious kingdom on earth, and so they were troubled by all this. Interestingly, Christ didn't answer their question directly but gave them signs in Matthew 24 and 25, things that relate to the Second Coming.

But it wasn't until the night before His crucifixion as He gathered with the disciples to observe the Passover and institute the Lord's Supper that He told them He was going to leave them. They couldn't believe it. This didn't fit their doctrine about a kingdom on earth at all. He said one of them was going to betray Him, and they had no idea it was Judas Iscariot. Then He said Peter would deny Him three times before morning. Their whole eschatology, their whole prophecy, was in shambles. What was happening anyway? It was all contrary to their expectations.

A WONDERFUL HOPE

It was in that context in John 14 that Christ for the first time in the Bible introduced the subject of the rapture of the church. The word "rapture" means "to catch up or snatch up," and it's what is described in detail in First Thessalonians, chapter 4. In John 14, Jesus recorded how He was going to leave His disciples, how He was going to heaven to prepare a place for them in the Father's house, and that He was going to come back and take them from earth to heaven. Nothing like that had ever been experienced before. There were Enoch and Elijah in the Old Testament, but no sizeable group went to heaven that way. This was totally beyond their comprehension, and He didn't explain.

That didn't come until later when the apostle Paul was saved and the Lord took him into the desert and gave him some post-graduate courses. Paul didn't understand the grace of God. He didn't understand the purpose of God to form a church of Jew and Gentile on the same basis by the baptism of the Spirit, and he didn't understand the doctrine of the rapture. But Jesus explained all this to Paul, and so Paul on his missionary journeys had two main subjects. One was that Christ died and arose again, and that people can be saved by trusting in Him. And the second message was that Christ is coming again to take you to heaven, and it could be any time. You know the amazing thing is that if you look up every passage on the rapture, there's not one passage that tells you to look for something happening *before* the rapture. It's always

> **There's not one passage that tells you to look for something happening *before* the rapture.**

presented as an imminent event, and that's still true. Regardless of when it is, it is now almost two thousand years closer than when Christ spoke these words. I believe it on the basis of certain evidences.

And so we have this wonderful fact that Christ is going to come, and in 1 Thessalonians 4, the apostle Paul explains the doctrine of the rapture in detail. Now it's not a difficult doctrine, but it's a doctrine about which many people who go to church regularly are ignorant because it often isn't preached. There are churches where you will never hear a message on prophecy, partly through unbelief, or partly through misunderstanding about it. But the people who are coming to church often do not know this wonderful truth: Christ is coming again.

Now, in 1 Thessalonians 4, Paul is answering certain questions. He'd been at Thessalonica for three weeks in his missionary journeys, and then had been forced to leave because of a plot to kill him. He had sent Timothy to see how they were getting along, and Timothy came back with a number of questions. One of the questions was what about people who had died? Some of that little band of Christians had already died since Paul left. The others wondered if the Lord came for the living, what would happen to those who died? Would they have to wait before they'd see them? And so Paul answers these questions and others, rejoicing, of course, that the Thessalonians were standing true to the faith in spite of all their persecutions.

He says in verse 13: "Brothers, we do not want you to be ignorant [uninformed] about those who fall asleep"—that is, those who die—"or grieve like the rest of men, who have no hope." What does that say? You either have a wonderful hope in Christ, or you don't have any hope at all. Now it's interesting

Paul calls them brethren. Fortunately, you don't have to know about the brethren to go to heaven, and I think when the rapture actually occurs, a lot of people who've never been instructed are going to be very much surprised. When they suddenly start rising from earth, it's going to be quite a shock. They may wonder what in the world is happening, but they're going to be raptured if they're saved. You're saved by faith in the first coming of Christ, not in the rapture, but the rapture is something God wants us to know about because He doesn't want us to face life with no hope when we lose loved ones.

> **He doesn't want us to face life with no hope when we lose loved ones.**

I attended a funeral one time of a little eleven-year-old girl who had died of leukemia. Her parents were prominent Christian workers. There had been a lot of prayer for years about her sickness and now she was gone. The church was packed with well-wishers, but it wasn't a time of mourning, it was a time of rejoicing. She was relieved. She was now perfectly well in the presence of Christ. She was rejoicing in her new liberties and those attending her funeral knew that someday, perhaps very soon, they'd see her again. I couldn't help but think, "What if she wasn't a Christian? And what if her parents weren't Christians? Then what?" What are you going to say? The Bible doesn't give us any leeway here. It's either a wonderful hope or no hope at all.

> **It's either a wonderful hope or no hope at all.**

Did you notice here in First Thessalonians 4 that Paul goes

on to say how absolutely *certain* this truth is? You know, we have a feeling that somehow prophecy isn't as sure as history. Well, there's an illustration where both are true. We believe that Jesus died and rose again. And so we believe that God will bring with Jesus those that have fallen asleep in Him. However, there was a time when the death and resurrection of Christ was prophecy. Now, of course, it's history, and he said if the death and resurrection of Christ is a certain item of our faith—and it certainly is, it's the very center of the Gospel—then we can also believe with equal certainty in the rapture which is yet to be fulfilled. Now, notice what he says, "We believe that God will bring with Jesus those who have fallen asleep in Him."

EXPLAINING THE RAPTURE

Now, what happens when a Christian dies? Well, a medical doctor can pronounce him dead, his life—evidence of physical life—is gone. But theologically a Christian dies when the soul leaves the body and goes immediately to heaven. That's what we believe. Second Corinthians 5:8 tells us that to be absent in the body, is to be present with the Lord. It's an instant transfer from earth to heaven. We can bury the body, but the soul is in heaven. Now when the rapture occurs, 1 Thessalonians 4 tells us that Christ is going to bring the souls of those who have died from heaven to the earth. And the purpose is stated in the verses which follow. He's going to resurrect the body, and the soul is going to re-enter that body permanently in resurrection. That is what is meant here by "He brings their souls back."

In the verses that follow, Paul describes a process that is not difficult to understand, even though it's supernatural. He says in verse 15, "According to the Lord's own word." Paul couldn't have gotten this from the Old Testament because it isn't there. There is resurrection there, but not rapture. But Paul had been taught this, and now he says, according to the Lord's instruction to him, that it is going to happen and that we, (that is Christians) who are still alive, and who are left till the coming of the Lord will certainly not precede those who have fallen asleep "for the Lord himself will come down from heaven, with a loud command, with the voice of the archangel and the trumpet call of God, and the dead in Christ will rise first. After that, we who are still alive and are left will be caught up," that's where you get the word rapture—caught up, or snatched up, or raptured together—"with them in the clouds to meet the Lord in the air. And so will we be with the Lord forever. Therefore, encourage each other with these words" (1 Thess. 4:16–18).

Now their question was: Would they have to wait to see their loved ones who had died? The answer is no, those who are dead in Christ, those Christians who have died, will be resurrected just a moment before. Living Christians are instantly changed as predicted in 1 Corinthians 15:51–53. In a moment, in the twinkling of an eye, at the last trump, we're going to be changed. And together we are going up to heaven.

Now why are the dead raised first? Well, the Bible doesn't say, but it's our custom to bury their bodies in the ground, and they have a little farther to go. So when they're resurrected, we join them, as it were, and meet the Lord in the air.

Suppose it happened tonight? It could, you know. People say, "When do you think the Lord's coming?" Could be tonight. We're not told when. But notice what's going to happen. The Scripture says the Lord will come down from heaven with a loud command. He's going to leave His throne in heaven and bodily come back to the earth. Now in His deity, He's everywhere present. But in His body He is in only one place at a time. He's going to come down into the air above the earth, and He's going to give a loud command, a shout. When that happens, all over the world, Christians will be instantly resurrected, and living Christians will be instantly changed into bodies that are suited for heaven.

Now, you all look pretty good to me, but there are certain things wrong about you and I don't have to have a theological exam to find out. What's wrong? Well, first of all we were born sinners, and we have a sin nature. Even after we're saved we still have it, and we can't go to heaven that way. We have to have a body that doesn't have a sin nature. These bodies of ours grow older, I can testify to that, and we can't have a body that gets older all the time in heaven. Also, our bodies are subject to death. It's amazing that we live at all when you consider all the hundreds of things that could cause instant death for our bodies. And we are mortal. So instantly we need a new body that's holy, without sin, that could be in the presence of the Lord, and rejoice in Him throughout eternity to come.

You notice this all happens when Christ commands it. The Scriptures record that not many days before Christ died, Lazarus died. You remember he was the brother of Mary and Martha, and they were very much beloved. Christ and the disciples often stayed in their home, which was on the eastern slope of the Mount of Olives. Christ was gone, Lazarus got sick, and they said, "Oh, if He was here, He could have healed Lazarus." They had seen Him heal so many. But He wasn't there. Lazarus died, and they had the funeral and placed him in the tomb.

When Christ came, He found them weeping because of their loss, and Christ shed tears too. Then He went out to the tomb, as you'll remember, and commanded them to take the stone away. Though they demurred, they finally did. And then He said, "Lazarus, come forth." What happened? Lazarus came forth. As one commentary puts it, "If He'd left off the word 'Lazarus' and said 'come forth,' why everybody in that area that was dead would have risen."

You see, the rapture's also going to be a *selective* resurrection. Not everybody's going to be raised at that time. Ultimately, everybody is raised, but not on the day of the rapture. And so when He gives that command, the rapture's going to occur. It's going to be accompanied by the voice of the archangel. The archangel is the head of all the holy angels, and he's been in the ceaseless warfare with Satan and the demon world. Satan has tried to hinder the Gospel, hinder Christians, and spoil their lives and testimony, and to some extent he's been successful. But now in spite of all that he has done, here is the church triumphant. We have victory on our side. And when that voice of the archangel sounds, Satan recognizes that victory.

And then there's the trumpet call of God. There are many trumpets in the Bible, but don't try to put them together. There are seven trumpets in Revelation; there's a trumpet in Matthew 24:31; there's a feast of trumpets. It is a signaling device that is used for various things much like we have a system of bells. This trumpet, according to 1 Corinthians 15, is going to be the last trumpet for the church. It's not the last trump of time. When that sounds, all over the world, we'll meet the Lord in the air, and then as He promised the disciples in John 14, He's going to take us to the Father's house. The rapture is a movement from earth to heaven. Unfortunately, just as there was confusion about the first and Second Coming in the Old Testament, there's some confusion today about the rapture and the Second Coming. But the two events are entirely different, and that's the way the New Testament presents them. The rapture is a move from earth to heaven; the Second Coming is a move from heaven to earth, when Christ is accompanied by all the holy angels and the saints. He's going to set up His thousand year millennial kingdom on earth, when He will reign out of Jerusalem over the entire world. At the end of that time, of course, the present earth and heaven will be destroyed, and the new heaven and new earth will be created, and in the new Jerusalem in the new earth, the saints of all

> **The rapture is the next event as far as prophecy's concerned.**

ages will spend eternity. That's our ultimate home, in the new Jerusalem in the new earth. And that's what's going to happen.

As soon as we meet Christ in the air, we're going to be with Him forever, like a marriage. That's the way it's described in the Bible. We're going to be with Him, and we'll be with the Lord *forever*. What an encouragement that is, what a comfort in time of sorrow for our fellow Christians who will depart, to realize that our separation may be short, and that any day Christ may come and we'll be brought together forever in the future.

WHEN WILL THE RAPTURE OCCUR?

It's a natural question, and is often asked. When will it occur? The Bible doesn't give us a direct answer to that. If you look up every passage on the rapture, you'll find that everyone has the same approach—nothing before the rapture. The rapture is the next event as far as prophecy's concerned, and of course that's the way it's presented in the Bible. Well, how can you know then, how can there be signs for the rapture if there are no signs for the rapture? It seems a difficult problem, but it really has a simple solution.

What we're seeing in our world today in a very *remarkable way* is the setting of the world stage for the events that will follow the rapture. Now if that's true, and I want to demonstrate that, then it's also true that the rapture could be at any time. We had an account in the Dallas papers about a man who did his Christmas shopping early. He was walking down the streets in November with his arms full of Christmas presents, and he met a friend who said, "My, Thanksgiving must be close."

You may laugh, but it made perfect sense, didn't it? Thanksgiving is a month before Christmas. If the world is getting ready for Christmas, and Thanksgiving hasn't occurred, then it means that Thanksgiving is impending, see? That's exactly our situation today.

In 1 Thessalonians 5, Paul goes on to raise the question of this day, and what he tells us is that the rapture begins the Day of the Lord. Old Testament books like Joel discuss the Days of the Lord. What are the Days of the Lord? They are any period of time when God deals in direct judgment upon His people. He would bring famine or pestilence or war against Israel when they failed and these were called "Days of the Lord." They could be more than twenty-four hours or for that period of time. The Old Testament itself also describes the future Day of the Lord you're going to hear about in the next chapter. That is going to be a wonderful truth for us to learn—what's going to happen in our world when our world is set up for exactly what's going to happen after the rapture.

It is always helpful for me to summarize what the Bible says about prophecy, and there are three great areas of prophecy in the Bible. One has to do with Israel, and the Old Testament is full of it. I don't see how modern scholars can say there's no prophecy about Israel because most of them have been fulfilled, but there are some that are subject to future fulfillment. And there's prophecy about the nations as in the book of Daniel about his four empires, Babylon through the Roman Empire. In the New Testament, there's also prophecy about the church.

In the last fifty years we've seen an amazing development in all these areas. First of all, after almost two thousand years of Israel's wandering over the face of the earth, in 1948 they once again constituted a political state. People sometimes ask, "Is prophecy being fulfilled today?" Why of course, every time you see a Jew walking, identified as a Jew, prophecy is being fulfilled because Jeremiah wrote many years before Christ that the Jewish nation would continue as long as the sun and moon endured. The sun's still up there; the Jews are still down here. There are no other people in the world who have maintained their identity over thousands of years like the Jew today, who knows he's a descendant of Abraham four thousand years ago. Who are your ancestors? Where were they a hundred years ago? Two hundred years ago? Not many of us have an answer because we are all blurred in America. Intermarriage has erased the lines of separation between countries, and now we're Americans. But a Jew is always a Jew, and that's what the Bible predicts. So there's going to be fulfillment of that.

Then, of course, the Bible prophecies of the end time also predict a world war leading up to the Second Coming of Christ.

> **Anybody who dates the rapture is going far beyond the information the Bible gives us.**

Since the Second World War, you have the United Nations, a world government leading eventually to a world war as the nations begin to rise against the leader of the world government at that time who is the Antichrist. And so we have these fulfilled things going on right now, but I can't date it; nobody can. Anybody who dates the rapture is going far beyond information the Bible gives us. Every year someone thinks they know, and there have been hundreds of attempts. You'd think they'd learn that they can't give a date, but people are still trying every year.

No, there's no way to date it, but we can say this, there's never been an hour in the history of the church when there's more likelihood for the rapture to occur any day. That's a theological fact, but it's a very practical fact, too, because it confronts us. The first basic question is, if the rapture occurred, would you be ready? Are you ready? Prepare to meet your God, that's what the Bible tells us, and certainly this is a very striking thing. In preparing to meet God, you have to realize that something supernatural has to take place in your life before the Lord comes and you are raptured. You need to be born again.

YOU MUST BE BORN AGAIN

I was brought up in a Christian home where we had morning devotions. My parents were prominent in the church, and we went there every time the door opened. At age nine I joined the church after passing five different catechism courses, and at age twelve I decided to be a preacher. At age fifteen, I had a shocking experience. I got into a class on Galatians, and in the second session I attended the teacher said, "You can't be good enough to be saved." That hit me like a bolt. After all I was doing everything right, wasn't I? I was going to church every time it opened, I was reading my Bible, I was praying, I was going to be a preacher.

> **We were saved by the Grace of God—not something we deserved, or earned, or attained.**

What more could you ask for? The teacher pointed out that no matter how hard we try, none of us is good enough to get to heaven. Nobody gets there on those grounds. Then he pointed out how God remedied the situation by His Son's dying on the cross for our sins, becoming our sacrifice for sin. When we accepted Him, then we were saved by the grace of God—not something we deserved, or earned, or attained—we were saved because we put our trust in Christ.

It's all so complicated on God's side to be sure, and so simple on our side. Christ said, "Him that cometh to me I will in no wise cast out" (John 6:37, KJV). But you don't get saved by joining the church; you don't get saved by education or morals or Christian life. Those are results, not causes. First of all, you need to be born again, like Nicodemus of old. You remember in John 3, he came to Christ by night and said he couldn't understand how Christ could be an evil man, like his associates had told him, and yet perform so many miracles. And Christ just cut him right down. He said, "Nicodemus, you need to be born again, or you'll never enter the kingdom of God." The wonderful fact is that you can. While Nicodemus had trouble with that, eventually he became a Christian and was one of those who prepared the body of Christ for burial.

But all of you have to be born again. Now Nicodemus was a good man. I think he was in the synagogue every Sabbath Day. I'm sure he paid his tithe. I'm sure he paid his offerings. He did everything right, you know, as far as he could. That's not the way to get to heaven. You get to heaven by the grace of God and the fact that Christ died for you.

> **You get to heaven by the grace of God and the fact that Christ died for you.**

Now if you haven't been born again, you're not ready for the coming of the Lord. No matter what else can be said about you, you need to be born again. When I first heard that, it jolted me. But I listened, and about a half a dozen sentences later the teacher explained in simplicity the Gospel that Christ died for me. I could be saved by trusting Him. I accepted it immediately. I can't understand why anybody would hesitate even for a moment when he's offered eternal salvation, forgiveness of his sins, and all the blessings of eternity in heaven. I accepted immediately. The next day, I knew something had happened to me. There was something stirring on the inside that wasn't there before. I was born again.

Unless you're born again, you're not ready. I'm afraid there are thousands of Christians, sometimes members of the church, who are living an outwardly Christian life, but not recognizing their need to put their personal trust in Jesus Christ as their sacrifice for sin and as their God and Savior. And that may apply to you. The first question is, Are you saved? Now, once you know you're saved, here comes the second question: What are you doing about it? One of the facts of Scripture is, if you're going to face Jesus Christ at the judgment seat after the rapture, and your life is going to be evaluated as to what we've done that's worthwhile from God's standpoint—and you have to face the fact that Jesus is going to be not only your Savior but your Judge—what are you doing with it? Are you leading a Christian life?

There are some Christians who don't manifest the grace of God in their life even though they're saved because they're not living as they should. How important that is to be saved and to be leading a Christian life where you're serving the Lord in every possible way you can.

THE PRACTICALITY OF THE RAPTURE

Now I believe the rapture is an important doctrinal subject, but it's most of all a practical subject. I find it's totally different if you believe the rapture could happen any day; some do not. I read a book one time that tried to prove the church had to go through the tribulation. I thought this theory was false, contradicted by the Bible. But I said, "Let's go along with it and not contradict every page." So I stayed with it for a couple of days. I suddenly realized that if I believed that this author was right, my total perspective in life was wrong. I didn't have hope; I didn't have even the coming of Christ; I didn't have the fulfillment of these wonderful prophecies. No, the Bible teaches that Christ is coming and He could be coming soon. Are you ready?

First of all, are you saved? Second, are you serving the Lord? These are practical, important, pivotal questions. It's not enough to listen, you have to respond. You don't have to believe if you don't want to, but if you're guilty of unbelief, you're going to pay the price that the Bible outlines for those who will not believe and accept what God has revealed in His Word. So may God speak to our hearts. May you be sure if the Lord came, you'd be ready.

Our Father, how wonderful it is to be saved, to know we're saved, and to be anticipating with joy that Christ is coming, perhaps even tonight. May this conference be confirmed by the fact that Christ is coming and we are in His presence forever and forever. Speak to anyone tonight to whom this may be new doctrine, something he hasn't heard before, been confused about. Somehow lead him to the place where he'll know he's saved by faith in Christ and that he's living for Him every day until He comes. For we ask in Christ's name. Amen.

DR. MARK BAILEY

The Tribulation

DR. MARK
BAILEY

Vice President of Academics; Dean of Faculty
Dallas Theological Seminary

DR. MARK BAILEY, pastor of Faith Bible Church in DeSoto, Texas, is Associate Professor of Bible Exposition, Vice-President of Academics and Dean of Faculty at Dallas Theological Seminary. He is also the author of *To Follow Him*, a book concerning the seven marks of a disciple. Dr. Bailey and his wife Barbara are the parents of two boys, Josh and Jeremy. They reside in Arlington, Texas.

CHAPTER
THREE

The Tribulation

Ed Dobson, in his bestseller entitled *The End,* has stated, "Hiroshima is a microcosm of what could and might happen. The current nuclear arsenal has the potential to wipe out civilization as we know it."[1]

Futurists Alvin and Heidi Toffler have written, "Nothing marks today's moment of history . . . more strikingly than the acceleration of change. This acceleration, partly driven by faster communications, means that hotspots can erupt into a global system almost overnight. . . . A small war in a remote place can, through a series of often unpredictable events, snowball into a giant conflagration. . . . We appear to be plunging into another Dark Age of tribal hate, planetary desolation, and wars multiplied by wars."[2] Does that ever sound familiar. Through Jesus we learn that wars and rumors of wars will abound.

Interestingly enough, of the two hundred members of the United Nations, sixty have waged war in my lifetime. That's one-third of them. The Tofflers put a pen to history and said, "In fact, in the 2,340 weeks that passed between 1945 and 1990, the Earth only enjoyed a grand total of three weeks that were truly war-free."[3] Did you catch that? In the last fifty years, there have only been three weeks of war-free experience on Planet Earth.

Dr. Harold Wilmington said it this way: "According to the Bible there is coming a calamity unlike any which this weary world has ever seen. And although this future period will be relatively short, it will nevertheless destroy more of this Earth's population than all previous disasters combined. The estimated toll of human life lost ranges from 750 million to one billion. An additional 340 million would be seriously injured, and 33 percent of those incapacitated because of radiation, chemical, or biological warfare."[4]

Jamie Peterson, who edited a book called *The Aftermath, Human and Ecological Consequences of Nuclear War,* said, "Should that war erupt now, the environmental toll includes massive water contamination, radiation fallout, toxic rain, uncontrollable fires and the resultant inability to grow food."[5]

Driving from Dallas Theological Seminary, I recently saw all the traffic blocked off on Highway 635 in North Dallas. I found out that I couldn't turn on Hillcrest, and I couldn't turn on Prestonwood. I had to go down by the Galleria Mall and circle my way back around. As I was listening to the radio station, I found out that ten thousand gallons of fuel had been dumped into the sewage system in Dallas. Can you imagine if that had happened worldwide?

Robert Reich of Harvard recently said, "We're living through a transformation that will re-arrange the politics and economics of the coming century. Each nation's primary political task will be to cope with the centrifugal forces of this global economy."[6]

CORE TEXTS FOR THE TRIBULATION

There is a series of passages that serve as a core curriculum for our study of the Tribulation. In Jeremiah chapter 30, beginning with verse 5, "This is what the LORD says: 'Cries of fear are heard— terror, not peace. Ask and see: Can a man bear children? Then why do I see every strong man with his hands on his stomach like a woman in labor, every face turned deathly pale?'" Don't miss the imagery, the metaphor of the birth pains. Jeremiah is obviously being very graphic. Since men can't bear children, why are they going to groan as if they were?

Verse 7 is the central verse, "How awful that day will be! None will be like it. It will be a time of trouble for Jacob, but he will be saved out of it." I want you to see two things in that passage. First, this is going to be one terrible time, obviously; but second, God will deliver Israel, who's called Jacob in this passage. Scripture records Jacob's name being changed to Israel. God will keep His promise to restore His people, Israel.

Daniel 12:1 states, "At that time Michael, the great prince who protects your people, will arise." Michael is the contending angel and Gabriel is the communicating angel on behalf of Israel. Gabriel was used to announce the birth of John to Zacharias and the birth of Jesus to Mary, among other tasks.

Michael, however, is depicted as the warring angel. And so "Michael, the great prince who protects your people, will arise. There will be a time of distress such as has not happened from the beginning of nations until then." Daniel sits at a fulcrum between Israel's past and Israel's future. Daniel sits within the seventy years of captivity in Babylonia. The seventy years were determined because of seventy "sevens." Four hundred ninety years of Sabbath years that were not kept by Israel determined the amount of time Israel would go into captivity and the land would lie fallow.

But Daniel also is the pivot between 490 years of previous history for which Israel was being judged and the 490 years of future history, the seventy "sevens" of Israel's future. Daniel says that there's coming a time in the future when there will be a time of distress that has never been known on Planet Earth before. "But at that time your people—everyone whose name is found written in the book—will be delivered." Notice two things about this verse. The terror of this time will be unprecedented, and every believing Jew is promised deliverance. "Your people—everyone whose name is found written in the book—will be delivered."

Joel echoes the warning of this tribulational time. Beginning in Joel 2:1 he says, "Blow the trumpet in Zion; sound the alarm on my holy hill. Let all who live in the land tremble, for the day of the LORD is coming. It is close at hand." What kind of a day is it? Joel 2:2 tells us it is a day of darkness and gloom, a day of clouds and blackness.

> **The terror of that time will be worse than any other holocaust the world has known or will ever know.**

Like dawn spreading across the mountains, a large and mighty army comes such as never was of old nor ever will be in ages to come. Joel parallels Jeremiah and Daniel, so to speak, as a pre-exilic prophet warning that the Day of the Lord will be a time of darkness. Nothing anyone can do will stop it. It will come regardless of whether people want it to or not. The terror of that time will be worse than any other holocaust the world has known or will ever know.

I love going to Israel. My colleague at the Seminary, Dr. Charlie Dyer and I love to tour together, and we've had many a trip where we've stopped together in Jerusalem at the Holocaust museum called *Yad Vashem*. It comes from the Hebrew words meaning a hand, *yād,* and a name, *vašēm.* It's an idiom, a hand and a name which together means "memorial." I remember the first time I walked through the Holocaust museum in Israel and was stricken with silence at the horror of what I saw. Depicted in graphic portraits, described in vignettes was the Holocaust of Eastern Europe. When I read my Bible and God tells me that there will come a time in the future that will make that pale in comparison, I must confess that I am moved inside at what it will be like.

Speaking of the last half of the Tribulation, Matthew quotes Jesus as saying in Matthew 24:21, "For then there will be great distress, unequaled from the beginning of the world until now." Don't miss that. That included the flood; that included the Assyrian invasion; that included the Babylonian invasion; that included the persecution of Egypt prior to that; that included the Medes and the Persians; that included Rome and their thumb on Israel. I take it that if Jesus were writing it now even post-Holocaust of our century, He would say the same thing, "Unequaled from the beginning of the world until now," and never to be equaled again. That's echoed again in Mark 13:19, in Mark's account of that Olivet discourse of Jesus.

THE NATURE OF THE TRIBULATION

Now with those basic passages laid down as sort of the core curriculum of what it's going to be like, I want to talk about the period itself. There are three great descriptions of this period to come on Planet Earth. One, it will be the worst hour of human history; two, it is called the Day of the Lord; three, it is called the Seventy Weeks of Daniel or the Seventy Weeks for Israel. In light of Joel chapter 2, it's the period after the Rapture. God has not destined us for wrath, but for the obtaining of salvation through Jesus Christ our Lord. Jesus promised in Revelation chapter 3 that there's an hour coming upon the earth, and the promise to the church in Revelation 3 is, "I will . . . keep you from the hour of testing that is going to come upon the whole world to test those who live on the earth."

The Worst Hour of Human History

It's the worst hour of human history for the world, and it's the worst hour of human history for Israel. Listen to a passage that relates to the world. Isaiah 24:3–6: "The earth will be completely laid waste and totally plundered. The LORD has spoken this word. The earth dries up and withers, the world languishes and withers, the exalted of the earth languish. The earth is defiled by its people; they have disobeyed the laws, violated the statutes and broken the everlasting covenant." That's what makes the judgment just. "Therefore, a curse consumes the earth; its people must bear their guilt. Therefore earth's inhabitants are burned up, and very few are left."

Dr. Dwight Pentecost highlights the Tribulation in his great volume *Things to Come,* and he notes the ten following descriptive words that characterize the period, all with appropriate scriptural support. Here are the words: wrath, judgment, indignation, trial, trouble, destruction, darkness, desolation, overturning, and punishment. He finishes his discussion with this statement, "No passage can be found to alleviate to any degree whatsoever the severity of this time that shall come upon the earth."[7] It will be the worst hour in human history for the world.

Three major convulsions are going to affect the world in general at this time. One of those is a *coming world government*. In the next chapter, Dr. Pentecost will discuss this and walk you through this coming world government, but needless to say if God were to fulfill His Scriptures in our day, in what's left of this century, it wouldn't take Him long to put it all together.

> We've never had a better setup for God to start the clock again. I don't think we've ever had the setup for prophecy to be fulfilled like it's set up today.

You might ask if I think that prophecy is being fulfilled today. I don't think we've ever had the setup for prophecy to be fulfilled like it's set up today. But if I read my Bible, Paul expected it in his day. "We who are alive and remain will be caught up together with them in the clouds" (1 Thess. 4:17). I think every generation should live as if it could happen today. We ought to plan like the Lord will tarry for a long time, but live in the purity of our lives as if Jesus Christ could come back today. Just listen to the kind of setup that could possibly mesh with prophetic expectations.

The modern European Union (EU) began when six nations signed the Treaty of Rome in 1957. These six were Belgium,

Germany, Luxembourg, France, Italy, and the Netherlands, with a combined population of 220 million people. In 1973, Denmark, Ireland, and Great Britain joined what was then called the European Economic Community (EEC), bringing 66 million more people into what would become the European Union. In 1981, Greece joined the EEC. In 1986, Portugal and Spain were added. Less than thirty years after the signing of the Treaty of Rome in 1957, the New Europe was 336 million strong. In 1995, Austria, Finland, and Sweden joined the EU bringing the total population to 362 million in fifteen member nations.[8]

You ask, "Doesn't the Bible talk about a ten-nation confederacy?" The answer is yes, but I simply state this to illustrate that it does not take very long—less than thirty years—for a block of power to develop that could influence the world.

Ed Hindson in his recent book said, "The significance of the new union treaty is that it set in motion Europe's desire to increase its international political force in proportion to its growing economical clout. It also sets in motion plans for a monetary union, including a central bank and a single European currency. No matter how it shapes up, the future means a New Europe. The philosophy of the New Europe is to form one cohesive market in order to compete on a global scale."[9] And if that wasn't enough for you, all you have to do is read the newspapers, or if you have stopped, just print out your investment results for the last thirty days and you'll understand how globally influenced your portfolio really is.

Along with a world government there is a *global economic control*, faster than we can even think about it. Within the nineteenth century, closely-knit networks of local economies were transformed into national economies. Today the national economies are being transformed into global ones. Initially, America led the way toward a global economy modeled on American capitalism, but today the New Europe is leading the way to a system that is often viewed as capable of setting the economic standards for the whole world.

Such ideas as "Buy American" are becoming less of a reality all the time. Robert Reich again notes that "when an American buys a Pontiac from General Motors, he or she engages unwittingly in an international transaction. For example, of $20,000 paid to GM, approximately $5,600 goes to South Korea for routine labor; $3,500 goes to Japan for advance components; $1,500 to West Germany for styling and design engineering; $800 to Taiwan, Singapore, and Japan for small electronic components; $500 to Britain for advertising and marketing services; and about $100 to Ireland and Barbados for data processing; the balance of $8,000 goes to manufacturers in Detroit, bankers and lawyers in Washington, and General Motors stockholders."[10] And you thought you were buying American.

This is a typical example of how the global web in economics already works. In time it will become even more complex. For example, Gilbert Williamson, president of NCR Corporation recently said, "We at NCR think of ourselves as a globally competitive company that happens to be headquartered in the United States."[11]

Forty percent of IBM's world employees are non-Americans. Big Blue has become Big Rainbow. Robert Reich notes that IBM Japan employs 18,000 Japanese workers, and with annual sales of 6 billion, it is one of Japan's leading exporters of computers. The question is whether it is an American or a Japanese company, or both.[12]

Whirlpool is even a more complex situation. It recently cut its American workforce by 10 percent, shifted production to Mexico, bought Dutch owned Phillips Appliances which employs 43,500 people in forty-five countries. Is it an American company because it has American headquarters, or because the majority of its stockholders are American? Or is it an international company that happens to be headquartered in America?[13]

Not only a one-world government, not only a global economic control, but there's also going to be an *overall apostasy* that infiltrates the world in this period called the Tribulation. I want to note that in 2 Thessalonians, chapter 2, Paul describes an ultimate apostasy of rebellion. He says, "Let no one in any way deceive you, for it will not come"—he's speaking of the day of the Lord as he's mentioned it in verse 2—"unless the apostasy comes first, and the man of lawlessness is revealed, the son of destruction, who opposes and exalts himself above every so-called god or object of worship, so that he takes his seat in the temple of God, displaying himself as being God" (2 Thess. 2:3–4, NASB). Dr. Pentecost will address his career and character in the next chapter.

If you let your eyes move down through this passage, and others of the Pastoral Epistles, you would find that this is called the secret of lawlessness, the work of Satan himself (2:9), and a powerful delusion (2:11). It is the big lie that will be believed.

In 1 Timothy 4:1–2, Paul says that this will be a period when people "will abandon the faith and will follow deceiving spirits." They will be deceived through "doctrines of demons" (NASB) through "hypocritical liars." They "will be lovers of themselves, lovers of money, boastful, proud, abusive, . . . unholy, . . . lovers of pleasure" (2 Tim. 3:2–4). Second

Corinthians 11:13 refers to "deceitful workers" (NASB), and Galatians 1:7 says, some "are trying to pervert the gospel." They will bring in destructive heresies, and they will practice shameful ways (2 Pet. 2:1–2). There will be deceivers (2 John 7), and they will be godless men and Christ deniers (Jude 4).

This is going to be an incredible period of wrath. But where does this wrath come from? What's the source of this destruction? If you said who's responsible for the Tribulation, we know that "Satan will fight against the nation of Israel" according to Revelation 12; "The beast will fight against the saints" according to Revelation 13, verse 7.

But as you do a study of the Scriptures, you will find that the predominate source of wrath mentioned without apology across the pages of prophecy, is God Himself.

> **The predominate source of wrath, mentioned without apology across the pages of prophecy, is God Himself.**

God is going to bring a righteous wrath upon the world, and God is going to bring a righteous wrath upon Israel. In later sections of this chapter I will discuss the seal judgments of Revelation chapter 6, the trumpet judgments of Revelation chapter 8, and the bowl judgments or the vial judgments of Revelation 16.

In each one of those sections believe it or not, all of those elements of wrath are credited to God Himself. He is the source of the seal judgments, called in 6:16, "the wrath of the Lamb."

The trumpet judgments are sent with the angels who have been around the throne of God as ministering spirits. They deliver the wrath of God in the form of the trumpet judgments in 8:1–2. In reference to the bowl judgments, Revelation 15:7 likewise tells us these are the accomplishment of His wrath.

Revelation 14:7 states, "He said in a loud voice, 'Fear God and give him glory, because the hour of his judgment has come. Worship him who made the heavens, the earth, the sea and the springs of water.'" Revelation 19:1–2 describes the Lord's Second Advent to the earth in that glorious Second Coming, "Salvation, and glory, and honour, and power, unto the Lord our God: For true and righteous are his judgments: for he hath judged" (KJV). This is one terrible period of time that will come upon the world.

The Day of the Lord

The period of testing is also going to a period of time that God will bring upon Israel. "There will be wailing in all of the vine-yards, for I will pass through your midst,' says the LORD. Woe to you who long for the day of the LORD! Why do you long for the day of the LORD? That day will be darkness, not light. It will be as though a man fled from a lion only to meet a bear, as though he entered his house and rested his hand on the wall only to have a snake bite him" (Amos 5:17–19). Now that's bad!

Imagine running for your life to get away from a lion, and then you meet a bear and run away from the bear. You get into your house and you're all tuckered out and breathing heavily. You slam the door and lean up against the wall and a snake bites you. You know you're having a bad day when . . . But that's what God said He would bring upon the nation of Israel.

Zephaniah, that little, three chapter minor prophet, in chapter 1 verses 14 and 15 says, "'The great day of the LORD is near—near and coming quickly. Listen! The cry on the day of the LORD will be bitter, the shouting of the warrior there. That day will be a day of wrath, a day of distress and anguish, a day of trouble and ruin, a day of darkness and gloom, a day of clouds and blackness.'"

It will be the worst hour on Planet Earth for the nations and for the nation of Israel. You ask why God is going to bring that. What's the purpose of the Tribulation? Not only is it the worst hour that's going to come on Earth, but over seventy-five times throughout the Scriptures, it is called the "Day of the Lord." "The day," "that day," "that great day." The major thought in almost all of these passages is the punishment or suffering for which God's wrath in judgment is poured out.

Now when you're reading in the Old Testament, or when you're reading in the New Testament, you must ask the question, to what does that passage refer? What is the reference to that particular reference of the Day of the Lord? Sometimes it has a near view. It is the judgment that will come by Babylonia on the people of Judah, for example.

Then there is the far view that we will see. But concerning the near view, Leon Wood—who is now with the Lord and was a great evangelical, premillennial, pretribulational scholar who has helped me greatly in Bible study from a number of his writings—has a great explanation of how this near and far view work together. He wrote in his book, *The Bible and Future Events:*

> In Old Testament text which pertained to precaptivity days, the occasion of suffering often carries both a near and a far reference. That is, two occasions are foreseen when the suffering predicted will be experienced. One in the near future and one in the distant future with the latter being more severe. The suffering of the near future is usually the Babylonian captivity and that of the far view is the Great Tribulation. Normally the text prophecies kinds

of suffering which were not fulfilled on the first occasion and this calls for some future fulfillment. Or the text may describe a glorious day following the time of suffering which was not fully experienced by Israel in her Old Testament return from the captivity, and this again calls for a future fulfillment.[14]

A second way that these references are used at times is what we call the far view. It includes a period of time. There are passages that relate the Day of the Lord to the suffering of the Tribulation as Leon Wood mentioned. But there are other Scriptures, like Second Peter chapter 3 and verse 10 that say that these scriptures include the blessings even of the Millennium. And so the far view of the Day of the Lord can refer to the period from the seven year Tribulation on through to the Millennium. And both are called the day, the Day of the Lord, that day. Zephaniah spoke of the judgment of that time, Peter speaks of the blessing of that time.

> **Zephaniah spoke of the judgment of that time, Peter speaks of the blessing of that time.**

But there's a third way in which it can be used and that's a specific day. It is the pinpoint day when the Lord returns. Now, let me take you onto a little bit of a fun avenue to sightsee. "The evening and the morning," Genesis says, "were the first day." The evening comes before the morning. Sundown begins the Jewish day. Sabbath in Israel starts sundown Friday afternoon and goes till sundown on the Sabbath. That's a little different than the way most of us think. Darkness comes before light.

Now if you look at the Day of the Lord, the first half of the day is the judgment, the second half of that day is the day of blessing. If you could take that day, and like a globe break it open in the middle, the specific reference that makes the difference between the darkness and light happens to be the coming of the S-O-N, who is also called the S-U-N of righteousness who will arise. He is called the Daystar, the Dayspring from on high. It is the Second Advent of the Lord that concludes this age and introduces the age to come.

> It is the Second Advent of the Lord that concludes this age and introduces the age to come.

In eschatology, in Jesus' view of the future, this present age culminates in judgment with the tribulational judgments, the last of which is when Jesus Christ comes out of heaven to gather the nations before Him. And the judgment of the sheep and the goats of Matthew chapter 25 takes place. It takes place at "the end of the age." That phrase is used throughout the parables of Matthew 13 to speak of the judgment that will come at the end of the Tribulation when the Lord returns and separates the wicked from the righteous. At the Rapture, it's the righteous who are taken and the wicked who are left behind. But at the Second Advent it's the wicked who are taken out and the righteous that are left behind. If it was a post-tribulational rapture and all the righteous are removed and glorified, then there would be no one to go into the Millennium in their natural bodies to procreate in the Millennium. That's a major problem with the post-tribulational view.

The reason is that the Lord comes back between the

darkness—Tribulation—and the light—the Millennium. And that's why the Day of the Lord can be used in a near reference to the cataclysmic events of the captivity, but more often than not it has a far view into the future, either the tribulational judgments, the millennial blessings, or the day of the Lord's return to Planet Earth.

Zechariah chapter 14 shows a quick vignette of this. One of the places that we love to stop when we visit Jerusalem is on the top of the Mount of Olives to set Scripture and prophecy in perspective. When we stand on the Mount of Olives, there is a Jewish cemetery that covers the western slope of the Mount of Olives and there is an Arab cemetery that covers the region just before the walls of the city of Jerusalem across the Kidron Valley. The reason the Jews love to be buried on the Mount of Olives is because of Zechariah chapter 14. "Behold a day is coming for the LORD when the spoil taken from you will be divided among you." In other words, they're going to get back everything that has ever been taken from them. "For I will gather all the nations against Jerusalem to battle, and the city will be captured, the houses plundered, the women ravished, half of the city exiled, but the rest of the people will not be cut off from the city. Then the LORD will go forth and fight against those nations as when He fights on the day of battle. And in that day His feet will stand on the Mount of Olives, which is in front of Jerusalem on the east; and the Mount of Olives will be split in its middle from east to west by a very large valley, so that half of the mountain will move toward the north and the other half toward the south" (Zech. 14:1–4, NASB).

Geologists tell us a fissure is working its way up underneath the Mount of Olives, but the only problem is, it's moving in the wrong direction. Jesus will not only go against nature at His Second Advent in terms of a supernatural bodily and physical return, but He will make the mountain split contrary to the natural fissure that's working its way up, which will create a valley. If you stood in Jerusalem and looked east, you'd look right through that valley out toward the wilderness.

Verse 5 states: "And you will flee"—that remnant who will be there,—". . . for the valley of the mountains will reach to Azel." If you have a Bible dictionary, go look up Azel and you'll find they don't know where it is because it's going to be a place of refuge. There are all kinds of theories, but if we knew where Azel was it wouldn't be a place of safety. Anybody could read it and find it. There are spots traditionally believed to be the location of Azel, but no one knows when it will be.

"You will flee just as you fled before the earthquake in the days of Uzziah the king of Judah. Then the LORD, my God, will come, and all the holy ones with Him!" Parallel that to Revelation 19: "And it will come about in that day that there will be no light; the luminaries will dwindle. For it will be a unique day which is known to the LORD, neither day nor night" (Zech. 14:5–7). Some of our students will figure that one out. They don't sleep at night because they're writing papers; they sleep during the daytime in class. There'll be coming a time when it will be neither night nor day.

"But it will come about that at evening time there will be light. And it will come about in that day that living waters will flow out of Jerusalem, half of them toward the eastern sea and the other half toward the western sea; and it will be in summer as well as in winter" (14:7–8). You can water ski and snow ski the same day in Northern Israel.

But the rest of the chapter talks about the Lord's coming and being king over all of the earth. And it's going to be a perpetual Feast of Tabernacles. Please understand it. It talks about Jerusalem. It talks about the Plain of Judah around Jerusalem. This cannot be a heavenly fulfillment. You have Jerusalem in the sight of Judah, with rivers coming out of Jerusalem to the Dead Sea on the east, to the Mediterranean Sea on the west. This is an earthly scene in which the Lord has returned to celebrate the Feast of Tabernacles. Whoever doesn't go up to Jerusalem to celebrate it, is going to be judged. This relates to the specific time when the Lord will land back on Planet Earth. Another designation for this time is the seventy weeks.

The Seventy Weeks of Daniel or the Seventy Weeks for Israel

"Seventy 'sevens' are decreed for your people and your holy city" (Dan. 9:24). Notice there are two concerns, the Jewish people and the city of Jerusalem. And there are six fulfillments that are going to take place in here according to that passage. These seventy 'sevens' are going "to finish transgression, to put an end to sin, to atone for wickedness, to bring in everlasting righteousness, to seal up vision and prophecy, and to anoint the most holy."

Daniel gives us the time frame, "Know and understand this: From the issuing of the decree to restore and rebuild Jerusalem until the Anointed One, the ruler, comes, there will be seven 'sevens,' and sixty-two "sevens.'" That makes sixty-nine "sevens." "It will be rebuilt with streets and a trench, but in times of trouble." Now the word for "sevens" is *šib ʿîm* in Hebrew, which can mean a week of years.

A good proof text for this is Genesis 29:27. Jacob works a week of years for his wife. And then he's tricked and has to work another week of years, but he gets Rachel at the middle of that period of time, and Leah. That's a great story. Beauty may go skin deep, but ugly goes all the way to the bone, and Jacob thought one was pretty and the other one wasn't. I urge you to read that story on your own some time.

Daniel 9:26 says, "After the sixty-two 'sevens,' the Anointed One will be cut off and will have nothing. The people of the ruler who will come will destroy the city and the sanctuary. The end will come like a flood: War will continue until the end, and desolations have been decreed. He will confirm a covenant with many for one 'seven.' In the middle of the 'seven,' he will put an end to sacrifice and offering. And on a wing of the temple he will set up an abomination that causes desolation, until the end that is decreed is poured out on him."

Again, there are two primary concerns, the Jewish people and the city of Jerusalem. But there are two princes, the Messiah and the prince of the people (NASB) who are to come. We can walk through the basic structure of this period of seventy weeks. There are seven weeks that begin with the commandment to go forth and rebuild the city, verse 25. There are sixty-two more weeks until the Messiah and the prince come.

For the mathematics that trace the sixty-nine weeks to a very particular day in the life of Christ, the so-called Triumphal Entry—the day of Christ's entrance into Jerusalem—I recommend the following books: *The Coming Prince* by Sir Robert Anderson. Alva McClean's *Daniel's Prophecy of The Seventy Weeks; The Chronological Aspects of the Life of Christ* by Dr. Harold Hoehner; and *Things to Come* by Dr. Dwight Pentecost.[15]

Jesus said in Luke19:42, "If you . . . had only known on this day what would bring you peace—but now it is hidden from your eyes." "He came unto his own, and his own received him not" (John 1:11, KJV). They missed the day of visitation.

After the sixty-nine weeks, there are two events that are talked about. You see them in verse 26. The Messiah will be cut off, and the city of Jerusalem will be destroyed. Now if that's all we had, we would understand that when Messiah the Prince shows up, there is the death of Messiah and then there is the destruction of Jerusalem. There is a gap. There is a gap between the sixty-nine weeks and the seventieth week. Some Bible scholars don't want to admit that there's a gap. But let me just tick off a series of proofs or evidences that will show a gap between the sixty-ninth week and the seventieth week.

First, gaps of many years occur in other verses of the Scripture. A basic few would include: Isaiah 61:1–2; Psalm 22:22–23; and Psalm 110:1–2. In other words, having gaps that require a period of history between two events sandwiched into one verse for summary purposes is not uncommon. This is true in the Old Testament and the New Testament.

Second, even in the text of Daniel, the sixty-nine "sevens" and the seventieth "seven" are removed from one another in the discussion. He says there are seven, there are sixty-two, and there are two events that come between those two. Then he picks back up in verse 27 of Daniel 9 to discuss the seventieth week. In addition, there are two events between these two that must take place. And by the way, between the death of Christ and the destruction of Jerusalem in A.D. 70, there's at least a thirty-seven-year gap. So the principal of the gap is established even by the history in its fulfillment.

Third, all the other prophecies in Daniel, especially Daniel chapter 2, chapter 7, and chapter 8, imply a gap. Toward the end of their visions, something is at work and then there has to be a gap in order for there to be a final fulfillment. It may be the stone that becomes the mountain kingdom that fills the whole earth in Daniel chapter 2. It may be the little horn in the Roman image of chapter 7. It may be the little horn in the goat imagery of Daniel chapter 8, the Grecian fulfillment. The latter probably is a prefigurement of Antiochus Epiphanes, who though he fulfills it in one sense, does not totally fulfill the prophecy.

In Jesus' Olivet discourse, the abomination of desolation is still viewed as future, and an ultimate fulfillment has to come. The six promises of Daniel 9:24 have not yet been fulfilled. Most would argue that the first three relate to the first coming, the last three anticipate a future coming. Those such as the amillenialists, who would interpret that there can't be a gap and you have to have a complete fulfillment in the ministry of Christ, have difficulty relating all of the events of the Olivet discourse as being fulfilled in Jesus.

> **The purpose of the Tribulation is to bring retribution on the world to punish sin.**

TWO PURPOSES FOR THE TRIBULATION

What is the purpose of the Tribulation? One purpose is to bring retribution on the world to punish sin. Psalm 2:6, "Then he rebukes them in his anger and terrifies them in his wrath, saying, 'I have installed my King on Zion, my holy hill.'" Revelation 3:10,

"Since you have kept my command to endure patiently," he says to the church, "I will keep you also from the hour of trial that is going to come upon the whole world to test those who live on the earth."

A second purpose of the Tribulation is to refine the nation of Israel to prepare her for the Messiah. Listen to Moses in Deuteronomy 4:30–31, "When you are in distress and all these things have happened to you, then in later days you will return to the LORD your God and obey him. For the LORD your God is a merciful God;

> A second purpose of the Tribulation is to refine the nation of Israel to prepare her for the Messiah.

he will not abandon or destroy you or forget the covenant with your forefathers, which he confirmed to them by oath."

We've quoted Jeremiah 30 verse 7 above: It talks about the time of Jacob's trouble. Zechariah 13:2 says, "'On that day I will banish the names of the idols from the land, and they will be remembered no more,' declares the LORD Almighty. 'I will remove both the prophets and the spirit of impurity from the land.'"

Zechariah 13:8–9: "'In the whole land,' declares the LORD, 'two-thirds of it will be struck down and perish; yet one-third will be left in it.'" Listen to his words. "'This third I will bring into the fire; I will refine them like silver and test them like gold. They will call on my name and I will answer them; I will say, "They are my people," and they will say, "The LORD is our God."'"

THE PLAGUES OF JUDGMENT

What will be the nature of the judgments, the kind of wrath that will come? This is probably one of the most worked-over sections, and so it is not my intent to spend a lot of time on it. I would encourage you to grab your Bible and move through Revelation and maybe make some notes along with the judgments. The last bowl, number 7, while it culminates in the Second Coming, has a storm with huge hundred pound hailstones that precede it. One thing I would encourage in your reading is to notice the storms that build in the Book of Revelation. Read through it and mark when the storms come. There's lightning and there's thunder, and then it gets bigger, then it gets bigger, and then it gets bigger. And notice how it culminates with the Second Advent of Jesus Christ. The Second Coming is the subject for the last chapter of this book.

I want you to see the structure of how these plagues parallel to the structure of Matthew chapter 24. It's my understanding that the seals that begin in Revelation 6 parallel the events of Matthew 24:4–8 and 24:9–14, taking you all the way through the Tribulation. When you open that last seal, it's the next "seven," which comes back and picks up near the midpoint of the Tribulation. The trumpets take you from there to the end which is the return of the Lord at the end. The Germans call this structure "the drag to the end" in which you have an overview that culminates at the end; then you have a return of a portion of that which culminates at the end. And then like the bowls, you have it emphasizing what's poured out at the end.

Matthew chapter 24 is a description of what the Lord predicts will come. I want to take you backwards to show you this. Look at verses 29–31 of Matthew 24 (NASB), "Immediately after the tribulation of those days," you have these cataclysmic signs in the skies: "the sun will be darkened, and the moon will not give its light, and the stars will fall from the sky . . . the sign of the Son of Man will appear in the sky, and then all the tribes of the earth will mourn, and they will see the Son of Man coming on the clouds of the sky with power and great glory. And He will send forth His angels with a great trumpet and they will gather together His elect from the four winds, from one end of the sky to the other." Here we see the Second Coming of Christ and the gathering of His elect.

Now jump back to verses 15–19. Remember I'm tracking you backwards. We come to the midpoint of the Tribulation. "Therefore when you see the abomination of desolation which was spoken of through Daniel the prophet, standing in the holy place, . . . then let those who are in Judea flee to the mountains; let him who is on the housetop not go down to get things out that are in his house; let him who is in the field not turn back to get his cloak. But woe to those who are with child." Now go through to verse 21: "For then there will be great tribulation, such as has not occurred since the beginning of the world until now, nor ever shall." The verse prior to that says, "Pray that your flight may not be in the winter or on a Sabbath." Why is the Sabbath an issue? Because you have God working with Israel to refine her in this tribulational period.

There are false Christs (verse 23) and false prophets (verse 24) Verse 27: "For just as the lightning comes from the east, and flashes even to the west, so shall be the coming of the Son of

Man. Wherever the corpse is, there the vultures will gather." This is the judgment that comes when the Lord returns, according to Revelation chapter 19.

After the Tribulation, the Lord returns as recorded in verses 29–31, "but when you see the abomination of desolation," when is that? That's the midpoint of the Tribulation. That's when the one who had made a decree for a week of years breaks that decree and exalts himself and brings an incredible wrath upon the nation of Israel. This is the abomination of desolation. Notice Jesus speaks of it as yet future. Antiochus Epiphanes could not have fulfilled it. He may prefigure it, but he cannot fully fulfill it. It is yet future from the time of the Lord. So we've gone from the midpoint all the way to the end, when the Lord comes.

Now go backwards with me to verse 4. This comes in response to a couple of questions the disciples asked in response to what Jesus said recorded in chapter 23:37–39, "'Oh, Jerusalem, Jerusalem, who kills the prophets and stones those who are sent to her! How often I wanted to gather your children together, the way a hen gathers her chicks under her wings, and you were unwilling. Behold, your house is being left to you desolate! . . . you shall not see Me until you say, "Blessed is He who comes in the name of the Lord."'" "I wanted to but you wouldn't," this was the contingency; "therefore your house is being left to you desolate," this was the consequential judgment; "you will not see me," there's going to be a delay until He returns. Within that context Jesus says, Jerusalem is going to go down and the disciples are asking, "When will these things be, and what will be the sign of Your coming, and of the end of the age?" (24:3).

73

Jesus begins to tell them in verses 4–8 not to be fooled. The wars, the famines, all are simply the beginnings of birth pains. Ladies, these are the Braxton-Hicks contractions. These are just the little signs to let you know it's starting to get close.

He said, "The end is not yet" (vv. 4–8). But look at verses 9–14. "They will deliver you to tribulation, and will kill you, and you will be hated by all nations on account of My name.

> **What you have in the seals, the trumpets, and the bowls in Revelation matches the structure that you have in Matthew chapter 24.**

And at that time many will fall away and will betray one another and hate one another. And many false prophets will arise, and will mislead many. And because lawlessness is increased, most people's love will grow cold. But the one who endures to the end, it is he who shall be saved. And this gospel of the kingdom shall be preached in all the whole world for a witness to the nations"— notice—"and then the end shall come." In verses 4–8, I take it, you have the beginning of the birth pains, not the great Tribulation. That starts in verse 9 and goes through verse 14. Jesus takes you all the way to the end, (24:14), then he comes back, picks up at verse 15 and takes you from the midpoint to the end. Then he takes you to the post-tribulational return of Christ to the earth in verses 29–31.

Why do I do this? Because I think what you have in the seals, the trumpets, and the bowls in Revelation matches the structure you have in Matthew 24. You have one series that takes you all the way to the end, the next one that reviews the second half, and then finally one that concentrates on the end.

This is a typical Hebrew way of arguing: Overview, restatement, and focus. And the focus of all three comes at the end of the age when Jesus Christ returns.

OUR OPPORTUNITY

I want to finish with a final plea. The Roman orator Cicero once said, "It is impossible to know the truth and not be responsible." We as evangelicals have the truth of Scripture, and we are in a position to be heard in America, even in the political arena, as never before. What was a point of influence and advice of the mainline denominations in the past has really come to the evangelical in recent years. But every Christian has an incredible privilege, as well as an incredible opportunity. I don't know of anything that gives me perspective for living in the midst of trial or the midst of joy like understanding the big picture.

> We as evangelicals have the truth of Scripture, and we are in a position to be heard in America, even in the political arena, as never before.

I want to finish with a favorite piece of mine from Billy Sunday, an evangelist of yesteryear whom my father introduced me to. He writes in a particular volume,

> Twenty-nine years ago with the Holy Spirit as my guide, I entered at the portico of Genesis and I walked down the corridor of the Old Testament art galleries where pictures of Noah and Abraham and Moses and Joseph and Isaac and Jacob and Daniel hung on the wall. I passed into the music

room of the Psalms where the Spirit sweeps the keyboard of nature until it seems that every reed and pipe in God's great organ responds to the harp of David, the sweet singer of Israel.

I entered into the chamber of Ecclesiastes where the voice of the Preacher is heard and into the conservatory of Sharon and the Lily of the Valley where sweet spices filled and perfumed my life. I entered the business office of Proverbs and on into the observatory of the Prophets where I saw telescopes of various sizes pointing to far off events, concentrating on the Bright and Morning Star which was to arise above the moonlit hills of Judea for our salvation and our redemption.

I entered the audience room of the King of Kings, catching a vision written by Matthew and Mark and Luke and John. I advanced into the correspondence room with Paul and Peter and James and John writing their epistles. And I stepped into the throne room of Revelation where towered the glittering peaks, where sits the King of Kings upon His throne of glory with the healing of the nations in His hands, and I cried out, "All hail the power of Jesus' name, let angels prostrate fall. Bring forth the royal diadem and crown Him, Lord of All."[16]

There's no way in one chapter that we can cover all of what the Tribulation will mean. But we've looked at some passages and we've looked at some principles. What God is going to do is bring upon the earth one of the most incredible judgment periods the world has ever known. There will be righteous judgment upon sinners, but God will be working. He'll work through some witnesses, and He will bring to Himself following the Rapture, 144,000 Jews and a great Gentile multitude all as one. He is at work bringing judgment upon His enemies, wooing the world again with one major final plea to come to Him. But the majority will not, and what they will face will make the Holocaust look easy.

The book of Revelation starts with a picture of the Judge before we ever have the picture of the judgments. When you come to know the Judge, the judgments will be viewed as right.

Would you bow your heads in prayer with me.

Lord, thank you for putting together both the beginning and the end of history. Thank you for being the Lord of all that's in-between. May we live holy lives which will attract others to the Savior and thus prepare us all for the future judgments you will execute upon the earth. To you be the glory. Amen.

DR. DWIGHT PENTECOST

The Antichrist: Who is the Next World Ruler?

DR. J. DWIGHT PENTECOST

Distinguished Professor of Bible Exposition Emeritus
Dallas Theological Seminary

DR. DWIGHT PENTECOST, is Distinguished Professor of Bible Exposition Emeritus at Dallas Theological Seminary and author of twenty books, including *Prophecy for Today, Thy Kingdom Come, Things to Come,* and *The Glory of God.* He has also served as book review editor of *Bibliotheca Sacra.* He has taught at the seminary since 1955. He and his wife Dorothy reside in Dallas.

CHAPTER
FOUR

The Antichrist: Who is the Next World Ruler?

The closer we come to the end of this millennium, the more the news media is introducing words such as Armageddon and Antichrist into almost daily conversation. I was quite startled this past week to hear one of the major corporations introducing their advertisement by referring to the trumpet judgments in the book of the Revelation. It's amazing that people are

> I doubt if there has ever been a time when people were not curious about the Antichrist.

focusing attention on these future events as though they could take place at any moment.

I doubt if there has ever been a time when people were not curious about the Antichrist. People in every generation have wondered who the Antichrist is, and they have picked out various individuals in their generation and speculate as to whether they could be the Antichrist. This is a prominent theme in Scripture, and it is a theme that has been selected for this chapter.

I trust you have your Bibles with you for this is a Bible study and we want to make use of the Word of God. I want to direct you to the thirteenth chapter of the book of Revelation.

John is fulfilling the role of a prophet, one sent by God with God's message to deliver to man. And in the thirteenth chapter, John introduces us to a beast. John uses many figures and many symbols to convey truth. To many these are mysterious, but they need not be, for when you compare Scripture with Scripture, you find that Scripture will interpret its own figures and its own symbols. So we are not left to idle speculation as to the significance of these.

Reading in chapter 13 verses 1 and 2 (KJV), "I stood upon the sand of the sea, and saw a beast rise up out of the sea, having seven heads and ten horns, and upon his horns ten crowns, and upon his heads, the name of blasphemy. And the beast which I saw was like unto a leopard, and his feet were as the feet of a bear, and his mouth as the mouth of a lion: and the dragon gave him his power, and his seat, and great authority."

Sea in Scripture is frequently used, particularly in the Old Testament, as a reference to Gentile nations. "But the wicked are like the troubled sea, when it cannot rest, whose waters cast up mire and dirt. There is no peace, saith my God, to the wicked" (Isa. 57:20). Such was Isaiah's condemnation.

The sea represented Gentile nations. John saw this beast emerging from among Gentile nations. He says a unique thing about this one at the end of verse 2: ". . . the dragon gave him his power, and his seat, and great authority." There's another symbol, the dragon. If you'll look back to chapter 12, the dragon is introduced to us there for the first time in the book of the Revelation. "The great dragon was cast out, that old serpent" and then that dragon is identified "called the Devil, and Satan, which deceiveth the whole world" (12:9). The dragon is the symbol for Satan. So here is one emerging from among the Gentile nations who receives his power and his authority and his right to rule, not from God who appoints kings and governors, but rather from Satan himself.

Then the description of this beast is given. What a strange beast it is. All we can say is it's a mongrel beast. Parts of it look like a leopard, parts of it look like a bear, parts of it look like a lion, and it's true you'll never see anything like this in any zoo anyplace in the world. This again is a symbol. What in the world is John talking about?

Now, again, a principle in Scripture is that if you want to understand a portion that's giving you trouble, you look for another portion of Scripture that casts light on that which is puzzling you. The best interpreter of Scripture is Scripture itself. And so I'm asking you to turn with me back to the prophecy of Daniel 7. We'll see many parallels between Revelation 13 and Daniel 7.

SETUP FOR THE FINAL GENTILE RULER

Daniel had been carried captive into Babylon in 606–605 B.C. He knew in studying Jeremiah's prophecy that God had announced that the people of Judah would remain in captivity in Babylon for seventy years to make up for the years that they had neglected God's Sabbaths—seventy for seven. And Daniel is turning over in his mind, "What's God's program for Israel now that Israel has been carried captive into Babylon?" In fact, when this vision was given to Daniel, the people of Israel had been in captivity for approximately seventy years. So as Daniel began to calculate from Jeremiah's prophecy of the seventy years, he concluded they were coming to the end of that period, and he was curious about what would come. What was God's program for Israel?

And God revealed Himself and His plan and His purpose. In verse 1 of chapter 7, "Daniel had a dream and visions of his head upon his bed: then he wrote the dream." And this is what he wrote: "And four great beasts," (verse 3) "came up from the sea." There's the sea again, the Gentile nations. Four beasts would arise from among the Gentile nations different one from another, four separate identifiable empires.

The first one was like a lion, verse 4. The second one, in verse 5, was like a bear. The third one, verse 6, was like a leopard. The fourth one, in verse 7, is described not so much from its external characteristics, as its internal character.

> **Each beast in Daniel 7 represents an empire that in turn would arise.**

And so we find here the beast of Revelation 13 is only an expansion and an enlargement of portions of what was given to Daniel so many, many centuries before. As we look again into Daniel 7, we're not left to scratch our heads as to the significance of these beasts, because it is made very clear in verse 17. And here God did not leave Daniel, either, to puzzle over this strange dream. He explained, "These great beasts, which are four, are four kings, which shall arise out of the earth," that is from among Gentile nations.

Now God is not picturing here just the individual leader, but He is uniting the empire with the leader so that each beast in Daniel 7 represents an empire that in turn would arise. The first one was like a lion. The unique thing is that eagle's wings emerged from this lion, and no one would have to interpret to one living in Babylon what empire this represented. If you go to museums in either Germany or London, you will find Ishtar Gates that were taken from the ruins of ancient Babylon and reconstructed in those museums.

Those gates were adorned with azure tiles, and placed in the walls surrounding or in the center of those azure tiles were winged lions. They did not write a road sign to travelers proclaiming, "This is Babylon," but when the traveler entered those gates, he realized that he was coming to the capital of the Babylonian Empire. And so Babylon would be the first of the four empires.

Babylon fell to a combination of two political powers, the Medes and the Persians. And that's why the second beast is a bear that's higher on one side than the other. This is a lopsided bear because while the Medes and the Persians united to overthrow Babylon, the Persians soon overshadowed the Medes. So in ancient history you don't study the Medo-Persian Empire, but rather the Persian Empire. That was the second beast here.

Then you come to the third, which is like a leopard. The unique thing about this leopard, its abnormality, was that it had four wings. Alexander the Great, leader of the Grecian Empire, defeated the Persians. After he had extended the Greek Empire from Macedonia all the way to the Indus River to the east of what is now Iraq, Alexander died when he was only thirty.

Since Alexander left no heirs, his kingdom was divided among four of his generals: Ptolemy, Seleucus, Cassander, and Lysimachus. Four generals each became ruler over a divided

Grecian Empire. Daniel will describe that in detail in chapter 11 of his prophecy.

He moves quickly on to the fourth beast. Now, if we can look for a moment in Revelation 13, John gives us the external appearance of this fourth beast. It was like a leopard and like a bear and like a lion. You will notice that John mentions them in reverse order, because Daniel is looking from his ancient historical perspective down through the corridors of time, and they appear first as lion, then bear, then leopard, and then the fourth. John is living under the fourth, so he is looking backward. So what's nearest to him, the predecessor? The leopard. Back of that is the bear and in back of that is the lion, so that John and Daniel are describing the same vision. And Daniel was told that Israel, during the course of her history would be controlled, dominated, ruled over, subjugated to four Gentile world powers. That was the sign of God's displeasure; it was a sign of God's divine discipline. God had made it very clear at the time of the return from Exodus, that the principle on which God would deal with His people was simple: Obedience will bring blessing, disobedience will bring discipline and possibly even disaster. And as He described that disaster in Deuteronomy 28, God said that He would deliver the people of Israel to the authority of Gentiles, and Gentiles would rule over them. They would not have their own king ruling in the royal city of Jerusalem. And here Daniel is told that four empires would rule in a time period that our Lord in Luke 21:24 refers to as the "times of the Gentiles." That is a very important prophetic statement.

The "times of the Gentiles" is that period in Israel's history when no Davidic descendant is ruling on David's throne over

David's people in the city of Jerusalem. It began with Nebuchadnezzar and it will continue until the return of Christ, when Christ will liberate Israel from her Gentile occupiers. And here in Daniel 7, we continue looking. After he's introduced the fourth beast, he introduces a very significant feature of prophecy. Look at the last words in verse 7 of chapter 7: This fourth beast had ten horns—a ten-horned beast. Again, Daniel must have wondered about the significance of that, but God didn't leave him to wonder, because when you look in verse 24 of chapter 7, it's explained. The ten horns out of this kingdom are ten kings in their individual kingdoms. Now the fourth empire obviously was the Roman Empire that came to power by overthrowing the Greeks. The Romans, as they swallowed up the territory that had been occupied by Greece, Medo-Persia, and Babylon, incorporated into themselves not only the land, but also the peoples, the cultures, the traditions, the laws, the customs, the religions of all these other peoples. That's why this fourth beast is such a conglomerate beast. Part of it Babylon, part of it Medo-Persia, part of it Greece, part of it Rome, but it had no relationship to the previous three. However, in referring to the ten horns, Daniel is given the history of the Roman Empire that would take place.

In fact it would take place almost half a millennium after John wrote the book of the Revelation. When the New Testament opens, Rome is at the zenith of its power, invincible, irresistible, dominate, controlling all things. But Daniel told us that there was going to be a division of the political power that had centralized in Rome among ten emerging nations.

Now this is spectacular. Where did Medo-Persia get its power? By taking over the political power of Babylon. Where did Alexander get his political power? By taking over the political power of Medo-Persia. Where did Rome get its power? By taking over the political power of Greece.

If Rome falls, and it did in the beginning of the fifth century, what would you have expected from the history of empires? That those who defeated Rome, would take over the political power of Rome, and constitute themselves as a succeeding political unity. That was the history of empires. But what's Daniel telling us? That political power of Rome would not remain united and become a fifth Empire, but it would be divided out among ten separate identifiable nations.

Now what happened? When the Huns and the Goths from central and northern Europe swept into Rome, at the beginning of the fifth century, they sacked Rome. They did not unite all the land that Rome had occupied under their authority, but rather many separate identifiable nations emerged. Nations such as Greece and Italy and Spain and Portugal and France and Belgium and Holland and Great Britain had their origin as independent nations through the break up and the division of the political power of Rome among these emerging kingdoms. So that fourth empire exists today as these independent nations exercise the political power independently of each other after the fall of Rome.

ONE-WORLD GOVERNMENT

Daniel now is going to carry on the history of that fourth empire and bring it to its ultimate conclusion. Let me point out to you that in Daniel 7:8, Daniel introduces us to a political leader who eventually will head up a reunited Roman Empire.

And even beyond that, as we shall see, a one-world government. As Daniel looked at these ten emerging kingdoms, there came up among them another little horn.

Now if each of the ten horns represents a king and his kingdom, we must conclude the little horn is another king who emerges from among the ten. He's called little because he had an insignificant beginning. Nobody paid any attention to him; he was inconsequential. But then he quickly gained power over three of the original ten horns. So you see one beginning to emerge as a political figure from insignificance. Nobody paid any attention, but now they begin to take cognizance of him.

This little horn is the subject of the rest of Daniel's prophecy from Daniel 7:8 to the end. Look at it in chapter 8, verse 23 where he refers to the "king of fierce countenance," same individual. In 9:26, he refers to "the prince that shall come," the same individual. Chapter 11, verse 36 says he is "the king that does according to his own will," or we can call him the willful king. In chapter 12, verse 11, he refers to "the abomination that maketh desolate." So over and over again, Daniel is enlarging on the work, the ministry, the activity of this one who emerges from among the nations that had their origin in the break up of the old Roman Empire.

Now go back to the book of the Revelation. If you look in 17:8, you'll find that John reintroduces us to the beast. This beast of 17:8 is the same beast of 13:1. And he says here that this beast that had ten horns, is the same one that Daniel referred to. Verse 12 says, "The ten horns which thou sawest are ten kings." Ten kings in their independent kingdoms. They're not united; they're divided. And John has to note that this beast has not yet come on the world scene, for he says they "have received no kingdoms yet." Now John was living under united Rome, not divided Rome. He was anticipating a division into the ten separate kingdoms, but he says that there will come one.

Revelation chapter 13, verse 13 states, "These," that is these ten separate kingdoms, "have one mind, and shall give their power and strength unto the beast." Now I want you to notice that this one who has been ruling over three of the ten is invited, is elected, is appointed, to be head over the ten nations that have existed as ten independent kingdoms, or ten independent horns, for an extended period of time—no clue as to how long.

Take one more step. And that's to go back to verse 7 of chapter 13, the first chapter we looked at. "It was given unto him to make war with the saints," that is, he becomes Israel's persecutor, "and to overcome them." Now, I want you to notice the last part of this verse. Power was given him, not just over the ten that have elected him: "power was given him over all kindreds, and tongues, and nations." In the book of the Revelation that phrase, "all kingdoms, and tongues, and nations," refers to international authority, international power. That's why I refer to it as a coming one-world government.

Now, Satan is not an innovator, he's an imitator. Satan knows full well God's purpose to enthrone His Son as King of kings and Lord of lords. God said in Psalm 2:6 that He had set His Son on a throne in the holy hill of Zion that's in Jerusalem. When that Son comes to reign as Isaiah 9:6 says, He will bear the name Prince of Peace. He does not come to power to rule in his earthly kingdom that John in Revelation 20 will tell us will last for a thousand years. He comes to speak peace to the nations, Prince of Peace.

SATAN'S IMITATION

We call this beast by a name that John never used of him, Antichrist. John, in his epistles, warns the believers there are already many Antichrists present. He is not talking there of an eschatological person. He is talking about the plan and purpose of Satan to deceive believers by promulgating a lie. But here we refer to this individual as the Antichrist.

> An antichrist can have two emphases from the Greek *anti*. It may mean "one who is *opposed* to Christ," or "one who comes as a *substitute for* Christ."

An antichrist can have two emphases from the Greek *anti*. It may mean "one who is *opposed* to Christ," or "one who comes as a *substitute* for Christ." Now those are not separate. They're interwoven, and this one who is coming is Satan's masterpiece of deception in which Satan will say to the world, "This one is your prince of peace. He can solve the world's political unrest, and if you submit to his political authority, he will institute a reign of peace here on this earth."

How does he do it? I'm sure you're familiar again with what Daniel wrote in Daniel Daniel 9:27, speaking of this little horn, "He shall confirm the covenant with many for one week," that is seven years. The "many" is a reference to Daniel's people, those to whom Daniel is delivering this revelation of God's disclosure of his program for the people of Israel. They will live under Gentile domination until the time comes when there will arise from among the nations that divided out of the old Roman Empire, a political figure who does not come to power as Nebuchadnezzar came to power by military conquest. Nor does he come to power as Alexander in Greece came to power by military conquest. Nor does he come to power as the Roman generals came to power and had themselves crowned emperor of the Roman Empire by military conquest.

This one will come professing to be able to solve the world's problems, and the first problem he attacks is, if I can put it in current terms, the Middle East Crisis, the conflict between Israel and the Arabs over Jerusalem. This one makes a covenant with the nation of Israel guaranteeing their peace, their security, their well-being, their welfare in their own land. When Israel receives that kind of a guarantee, Israel joins herself with the beast, with this little horn, this prince that shall come, and becomes in effect an eleventh horn in that federation. Do you see the satanic deception? What do the people of Israel want and need today more than anything else? Secure borders, peace, freedom from terrorism. What does this one promise them? If you put yourself under my protection, then I will guarantee all these things. And Israel in her hardness and coldness of heart says, "This must be our Messiah, this is our Christ." But he is anti-Christ, opposed to Christ, and as a substitute for Christ.

I see the first part of this individual as a political ruler, imitating the reign of Christ because when Christ returns to this earth the second time to rule and to reign, He unites all kingdoms under His authority, and that's Revelation 11:15: "The kingdoms of this world are become the kingdoms of our Lord, and of His Christ; and He shall reign forever and ever." But all this is an imitation of what God has purposed for His people, for this earth.

ONE-WORLD ECONOMY

Revelation 13:16–17 states: "He causeth all, both small and great, rich and poor, free and bond, to receive a mark in their right hand, or in their foreheads: And that no man might buy or sell, save he that had the mark or the name of the beast, or the number of his name." What I'm suggesting here is that when this one becomes head of a one-world government, he institutes a one-world economy. That's the simplest

> **When this one becomes head of a one-world government, he institutes a one-world economy.**

way I know to put it, a one-world economy. And he demands not only absolute submission to his political power, but absolute submission to his economic authority as well, so that no one can buy or sell anything unless he has the sign of submission to his authority.

Now why is this so crucial? If you look back in Revelation chapter 6, we have a record there of the first series of judgments that God will pour out during the tribulation period. And the third judgment comes in verse 6: "A measure of wheat for a penny, and three measures of barley for a penny; and see thou hurt not the oil and the wine." Remember from our Lord's parable in Matthew 20 that the one who hired people to work in his fields agreed to pay them a penny or denarius a day. It was a silver coin that was used to pay a working man's wage for a day's labor.

And what it says here is that the economic situation has become such that it will take all that a man can earn in a day to purchase one measure of wheat. Now wheat was a grain normally used to bake bread, and bread was the staple of the people's diet. A measure of wheat would provide a day's bread for a family of four. And John says the situation has become such that it will take all a man can earn in a day to provide a crust of bread for his family.

But he can buy three measures of barley for a day's wage. Barley was such a coarse grain it was normally used to feed cattle. The poorest made their bread out of barley. That's why it's significant that the lad who brought his little loaves and gave them to Jesus, offered Him barley loaves, indicating a very poor family. What this is saying is that the economic system will be so out of control, that if one has to spend money for something besides food, his family will be reduced to eating cattle food.

> **If Satan is to deceive the world that his puppet is Messiah, he's going to have to control the economy.**

Now along with the bread, there was always olive oil in which people could dip their bread. They didn't use butter, the bread was dipped in olive oil and was washed down with wine. John says the economic situation will be so severe, don't even consider trying to have olive oil for your bread or wine to wash it down with, because it won't be available. This is a chaotic economy.

When Christ comes, what's going to be the situation? There will be no hunger, no famine, no poverty, no want. The hills will drip with new wine. The fields will produce bountifully—so bountifully, that before a man is done sowing, the reaper will be there to cut them. What a picture of unprecedented prosperity! And if Satan is to deceive the world that his puppet is Messiah, he's going to have to control the economy. How does he do it? By demanding that all who are in his system to submit themselves to the system that he can tell them what they can buy, where they can buy it, how much they pay for it, how much they can sell of what they have. Controlled economy, how interesting.

I was talking with one of our board members recently. He told me that his son, a student in Stanford, has been working with the think tank of IBM for the last two summers . And he said that several months ago ABC, on the evening news, relayed the information that the think tank had designed a very, very small chip, that could be inserted under the palm of the hand, so that the energy from the body would transmit information from that chip to a doorknob. That doorknob could be set

One would have to be blind, deaf, and dumb not to realize that Washington is surrendering a great deal of its authority to the United Nations.

up to determine its response to that chip, so it could admit or exclude simply by the touch of the hand. It didn't have to be implanted; it could be on a card carried in a pocket, or put into the heel of the shoe. It's not difficult to see how that ability could easily be extended so the cashier at the grocery counter could determine what you could buy and how much you'd pay for it.

You think we're headed toward one-world government? One would have to be blind, deaf, and dumb not to realize that

Washington is surrendering a great deal of its authority to the United Nations. The United Nations is a voluntary union of nations to form a political power. You think we're headed toward a one-world economy?. How many of you drive Japanese cars? How many of you watch a Japanese TV? How many of you have Japanese telephones? What's happened? A developing one-world economy means we're depending on other nations to provide what historically we'd always provided for our own people. We're moving toward a one-world economy.

ONE-WORLD RELIGION

That isn't all. I see another thing in Revelation 13:8: "All that dwell upon the earth shall worship him." Verse 7 has told us that the whole earth has come under his political authority. So, worship whom? This little horn, this beast. He will introduce a one-world religion. John is describing this little horn, the one whom Jesus called in Matthew 24:15, "the abomination of desolation." Paul calls him in 2 Thessalonians 2:3, "that man of sin," "the son of perdition" or "the man of lawlessness" (NASB). All are the same individual, the Antichrist. And Paul is not referring here to his one-world government, or his one-world economy, but rather his one-world religion, because in verse 4, he "opposeth and exalteth himself above all that is called God, or that is worshipped; so that he as God sitteth in the temple of God, shewing himself that he is God."

Whom did Jesus Christ claim to be when He came? God come in the flesh. What will this one claim to be when he has assumed the political authority that rightly belongs to Christ and has instituted a one-world government? And when he has taken the blessing that Christ promises to provide prosperity and plenty in a one-world economy, he then becomes the object of worship, representing himself as God come in the flesh.

How does this happen? Again we look in Revelation 13. We're introduced in verse 11 to a second beast. The second beast is not a political ruler, he's not an economic czar; he rather is a religious leader because he has two horns like a lamb, and the lamb from the Old Testament was the symbol of the heart of

> **Satan has power to duplicate miracles. He can perform miracles, but he does not have the power to give life.**

the Levitical system, the sacrifice of animals to God. This is a religious leader. What is his role? Verse 12: "He causeth the earth and them which dwell therein"—who are already under the political and economic authority of the beast—"to worship the first beast."

This first beast had a deadly wound that had been healed. Now this is a mystery to me and I don't profess to be able to answer it. But I see this as an imitation of the resurrection of Jesus Christ.

What is the evidence that Jesus Christ is who He claimed to be, the Son of God? He was raised by the power of the Father on the third day. And there is evidently a simulated resurrection that says this one is God. And this second beast, this religious leader, points to men and demands that they worship the first beast. How does he do it?

You can remember from your study of the Gospels that when Christ claimed to be the Son of God, He proved it by doing what only God could do. He healed the sick, restored sight to the blind, unstopped deaf ears, made paralytics walk, raised men from the dead. Every miracle that Jesus performed was an authentication of His claim that He is God. This false prophet will perform miracles by Satan's power. Satan has power to duplicate miracles. Satan's emissaries did that in the days of Moses when they duplicated the miracles of God before Pharaoh. He can perform miracles, but he does not have the power to give life. That's why I take it this Antichrist is not a resurrected individual, but one who has simulated resurrection.

Further, "he doeth great wonders, so that he maketh fire come down from heaven on the earth in the sight of men" just like Elijah. He "deceiveth them that dwell on the earth by the means of those miracles he had power to do in the sight of the beast; saying to them that dwell on the earth, that they should make an image to the beast, which had the wound by a sword, and did live." He performs miracles to convince the world, those that are under his political and economic authority, that they should recognize him as God. That's why Paul writes, "He as God sitteth in the temple of God shewing himself that he is God" (2 Thess. 2:4).

Now how's all this going to come about? Nations don't usually act independently or involuntarily. There's a manipulation going on behind every decision that every political ruler makes. And when I look in Revelation 17, I see that John says he saw the beast, this same beast, this politico-economic, religious dictator. And he saw a strange thing. There is a woman astride the beast, sitting in the saddle if you please. Now even my friend who comes from South Carolina has been in Texas long enough to know that the one who's in the saddle is in control over that which he's riding. So this woman is pictured as being in control over the beast.

What's she doing? She's working out her will in the politico-religious realm to get this one whom we named Antichrist to follow her plans, her purposes, her designs. She's called "Babylon" and in the next chapter you're going to be taken by a specialist in this area, Dr. Charlie Dyer, into Babylon and its place in prophecy. I'll just mention that Babylon was the center, the origin, of the first false religious system that ever existed. There had been unbelief before Genesis 11. But there had never been an organized religious system. And in Babylon, a woman emerged who took to herself the High Priestess, the Queen of Heaven, the Mediator between men and God, the one through whom men could have access to God, and the symbol of her religion was a mother cradling a babe in her arms. It's known historically as the Mother-Child cup that passed from Babylon into Pergamum where, John writes in Revelation 2:13, Satan's throne is. And it passed from there under Roman domination, into Rome itself, where you had the worship of Venus and Cupid. But after Constantine in 312 declared

This one-world religion sets Jesus Christ aside and offers men a false hope.

Christianity the official religion of the Roman Empire, he changed the names of Venus and Cupid to Mary and Jesus. Rome became the center of a religious system that offers access to God, not through the crucified son, but through the mother, the Queen of Heaven.

One who occupies that throne today, said this last week, he hoped to live to the year 2,000—to the new millennium—

because he proposed to bring peace to the Middle East through the exercise of the authority of his office. This one-world religion sets Jesus Christ aside and offers men a false hope. It directs men to a false God, false king, a false provider. This is worthy of an entire study in itself. But what I'm suggesting is that we can see movements in the political realm, in the economic realm, in the religious realm that are preparing the way for the advent of this little horn, this beast that John writes about so graphically in Revelation 13.

OUR RESPONSE

The Antichrist's coming cannot be until after the believers of this age are translated into glory. You're wasting your time trying to figure out if a certain political ruler either in Washington or London or Berlin is the Antichrist. It's foolish. He will be revealed only by making a covenant with Israel. That takes place after you and I are in glory. But if we can see that world movements are preparing the way for the coming of this one, we can't help but draw the conclusion that the coming of our Lord is drawing nigh.

Will you imagine please, a platform that is shut off by a curtain that's drawn? There's a lot of activity going on behind that drawn curtain. If there's a little crack between the bottom of the curtain and the floor, you can see feet rushing around, you can hear furniture being moved, you can hear things going on. You can't see, but you know that the stage manager is in control and is directing to make sure that every person and every prop essential to that drama is in place.

I think that's the day in which we're living. The one who

designed all human history and showed us how it will culminate in the enthronement of Jesus Christ as King of kings and Lord of lords is getting the stage set. And the only thing that keeps that curtain from going up is the stage manager. He is just looking over, making sure everything is set, and in His appointed time He'll say lift the curtain. That'll be when we're translated into glory and this drama will unfold.

Our Lord in Matthew 24:42–45, as He gave warning to the believers concerning His coming, gave them three exhortations: be watching, be ready, be faithful. And if you believe that the curtain is ready to be lifted, those are exhortations which you should heed. May I say there's only one way in which you can be prepared to meet our Lord at His coming, and that is to receive Jesus Christ as your personal Savior. God stands to offer to you His love gift. His love gifts are forgiveness of sins, eternal salvation, bringing you into His family as His beloved child. Those are His gifts. How does any gift that is offered you become yours? You simply believe that the offer was genuine, you take it, and say, "Thank you." I invite you if you do not know Christ personally, to prepare for His coming by receiving His gifts.

He didn't say be watching for Antichrist, but be watching for the One whose name is above every name, before whom every knee shall bow and every tongue confess that He is Lord, to the glory of God the Father (Phil. 2:9–11).

Father give us joy in hearing, joy in understanding, joy in believing, joy in responding. In Jesus' name we pray. Amen.

DR. CHARLES DYER

Babylon: Iraq and the Coming Middle East Crisis

DR. CHARLES
DYER

Executive Vice President
Dallas Theological Seminary

D R. CHARLES DYER is Executive Vice President of Dallas Theological Seminary where he has served since 1976. Besides being a frequent contributor to Bible commentaries and to *Bibliotheca Sacra,* the Seminary's theological journal, Dr. Dyer has co-authored and written many books, including *The Rise of Babylon, World News and Prophecy,* and *Israel Study Guide.* He and his wife Kathy live in Garland, Texas, with their two children.

CHAPTER

FIVE

*Babylon: Iraq and the Coming
Middle East Crisis*

We're going to go from the United States to Iraq and from Genesis to Revelation. So we're going to be hitting the ground running and moving rapidly as we head through God's Word.

The first thing I want to do is take you with me to Iraq. I'm sure it's a place that's always been on your "must-see" list for your itinerary in life. I will describe some of the sites, and then I will come back to look at God's Word and see if there's significance in what we have seen.

Driving down a road in Iraq, you can see a giant portrait of Saddam Hussein. It's like a "Welcome to Dallas" sign, except they do the welcome signs with his picture. His picture is everywhere in Iraq. He has influenced that country, and he exploded on the world scene in 1990 when he invaded Kuwait. I was in Iraq in 1987 and again in 1988 for the Babylon Festival. Most people don't realize that Saddam Hussein started rebuilding the city of Babylon shortly after he became ruler in Iraq in 1979. Eight years after that he held his first Babylon Festival. One poster was every-where through Baghdad. It shows a portrait of two individuals. The first is Saddam Hussein; the other is Nebuchadnezzar. If you could compare Saddam Hussein with Nebuchadnezzar, looking carefully at the eyes, the nose, and the lips, you would notice a similarity. Saddam Hussein had the poster drawn so that he and Nebuchadnezzar looked alike.

Since 1979 Saddam Hussein has been rebuilding the city of Babylon on its original foundations.

His goal in holding the Babylon Festival was to wrap himself in the mantle of Nebuchadnezzar and the glories of ancient Babylon and to pro-mote what he wants to do with the nation of Iraq today. Most people think there's nothing left of Babylon, that the Bible says it should just be a haunt of jackals. No one can live there; no Arab will pitch his tent there. That's the view many people have of Iraq and Babylon. And in fact, parts of Babylon itself are still in ruins, just the bricks from a bygone time.

But since 1979 Saddam Hussein has been rebuilding the city of Babylon on its original foundations. While the foundation is still covered in sand in some places, the walls of Babylon are going up right beside them in others. The bricks at the bottom of the city were laid by Nebuchadnezzar twenty-five hundred years ago. It's an archeologist's nightmare, but Saddam Hussein is trying literally to build on the original foundations laid by King Nebuchadnezzar two and a half millenia ago.

Procession Street is the main street leading into Babylon. When I was there for the opening night of the Babylon Festival, they had a cast of thousands march down this street dressed as ancient Babylonian soldiers promoting the rebirth of this city under Saddam Hussein.

Some of the temples and other buildings have been rebuilt. One of the temples, called the Ninmach Temple, was rebuilt on its original foundations. It is only one of several that were open when I was there, and it's in the portion of the city of Babylon that's been restored.

In 1987, all that was left of Nebuchadnezzar's Palace were just some scattered ruins and the gateway. The throne room had been rebuilt, but nothing else. One year later, the walls were entirely rebuilt around Nebuchadnezzar's Palace. In one year's time, over two-thirds of that palace had been restored.

Hussein finished the remainder of Nebuchadnezzar's Palace before the Gulf War. Even more exciting, Saddam Hussein has built one of his many palaces in Babylon on a hill constructed beside Nebuchadnezzar's Palace. Actually, Hussein has two palaces in Babylon and many others throughout Iraq. He built his palace so he could look down on Nebuchadnezzar's palace.

Another dwelling place that Saddam Hussein has in Babylon is called the Saddam Hussein Guest House. It's where I went in 1987 and 1988 as the guest of the government of Iraq. We held meetings there as Hussein glorified this great city that he was rebuilding and again wrapped himself in the mantle of King Nebuchadnezzar. This building, by the way, is right next to the Euphrates River which to this day flows through Iraq and right through the heart of ancient Babylon. The Euphrates River is still there.

The one thing that's not dated from the time of King Nebuchadnezzar is a theater. It was built by Alexander the Great.

He was rebuilding Babylon as the eastern capital for his empire when he died in the city. This theater was used for the opening night of the Babylon Festival. The performance began with some music and ended with a tribute to Ishtar, the mother goddess of Babylon, who was credited with bringing this eternal city back. A man bowed down before a woman who represented Ishtar as the words in French and Arabic and English extolled this eternal city's return under Saddam Hussein.

The city was never damaged in the Gulf War, and as soon as the war was over, Saddam Hussein continued building. Every September he holds the Babylon Festival, extolling what he's doing to rebuild the city of Babylon.

What gives Babylon significance, if it has any, is the Bible. And that's where we want to spend the rest of this chapter, going from Genesis to Revelation to look at a topic that most don't know is a thread that weaves its way through the Bible. I want to trace that thread with you, as it's woven by God into His book. Hopefully when we finish, you'll understand the significance of those places and the significance of a larger portion of God's Word.

> **Babylon was the first center started after the Flood, and it was started by a man whose very name means, "rebel."**

BABYLON'S REBELLIOUS RISE

Let's turn first to Genesis 10, which has all the hard names of the Bible no one can pronounce, the Table of Nations. It is significant as you get into the Table of Nations, where the Lord traces the descendants of Noah, that there's one individual named Nimrod whose name sounds like the Hebrew word *"marad"* which is the word for rebel. Genesis 10:8–9 says that he was "a mighty warrior on the earth. He was a mighty hunter before the LORD," and they had an expression, "like Nimrod, a mighty hunter before the LORD."

In verse 10, the first centers of his kingdom were listed, and the first city built following the Flood is Babylon. Babylon was the first center started after the Flood, and it was started by a man whose very name means, "rebel." It also says he built some other cities, "Erech, Akkad and Calneh in Shinar." Shinar is what we would know today as southern Iraq, that alluvial plain south of Baghdad. Shinar is the region, Babylon is the city, Nimrod is the founder, and it's the first city built following the Flood.

Now look at Genesis 11, a chapter we know so well that sometimes we miss the details. Verses 1–2 say, "The whole world had one language and a common speech. As men moved eastward," and we have to ask a question. Who's moving them eastward? Who is leading them as they travel to the plain of Shinar and settle there? The previous chapter told us who it is. It's Nimrod.

Nimrod is leading all of humanity eastward where "they found a plain in Shinar and settled there" at the town of Babylon. Verses 3–4: "They said to each other, 'Come, let's make bricks and bake them thoroughly.' They used brick instead of stone, and tar for mortar. Then they said, 'Come, let's build ourselves a city, with a tower that reaches to the heavens, so that we may make a name for ourselves and not be scattered over the face of the whole earth.'"

That verse is the key to understanding Babylon in the Bible.

The first city built by humanity following the Flood had a purpose. In fact, let me give you three reasons that I think describe why this city and this tower were built. They said, "Come let us build ourselves a city, with a tower that reaches to the heavens."

They Wanted Salvation

People wonder why they built this tower. Was it for astrology or astronomy? Was it as a rallying point? All those are possible, but the biblical text indicates their thinking was, "We're here on earth, God is in heaven, we're going to work our way to God. We're going to build a tower that gets us from where we are to where we want to be. We want salvation, we want to find a presence with God, and we're going to do it our way." These people wanted to build a tower that would get them to heaven.

> If I can get to heaven on my own, then I can get to God and say, "Look how good I am. I deserve to be here, I made it on my own."

The very next verse says, "The LORD came down to see the city" (Gen. 11:5). Now that's not because God has eyesight something like mine. The text is written that way to show that though they thought they could get to heaven, their efforts fell so pitifully short, God had to leave heaven to come down to see what they were doing. Now that shouldn't surprise us.

Go any direction from where you are. Pick a house at random, knock on the door, and ask that person, "How do you get to heaven?" Most people will say something like, "Well, if I'm good enough, don't kick the dog, treat my spouse right, try to be nice to my kids, then at the end of my life, if my good works outweigh my bad, I hope to get to heaven."

My friend, if that's what you think, you need to remember what happened in Babylon. They thought they could build a tower that could get them to heaven. They thought they could obtain salvation on their own, but their works fell short. Just like the apostle Paul says, "All have sinned and fall short of the glory of God" (Rom. 3:23). They wanted salvation, but they wanted it on their own terms. Why?

They Wanted Significance

"So that we may make a name for ourselves" (Gen. 11:4). You see, if I can get to heaven on my own, then I can get to God and say, "Look how good I am. I deserve to be here, I made it on my own." They wanted significance, but they wanted it for their own prideful motivation. They wanted to make their own name great.

In the very next chapter in Genesis, God summoned Abraham and said to him, "I will make your name great" (12:2). Greatness comes from being in a right relationship with God. But these people wanted to make their own name great. They wanted salvation, "We're going to get to heaven on our own." They wanted significance, "We'll make our own name great."

They Wanted Security

They wanted to do all this lest they "be scattered over the face of the whole earth" (Gen. 11:4). A need to feel secure is a common theme for everyone throughout the ages. But you have to understand, God had already given them a command to be fruitful, multiply, fill the earth (Gen. 9:7). What God had intended for good, they saw as a threat, and they said, "We don't like your plan, God, we've got a better one. It's ours. We're going to stay together and that's where we'll find our security. We won't be scattered across the face of the earth."

> **From this point on, Babylon has a character; it's a city of pride and rebellion that shakes its fist at God.**

Babylon is the first city built following the Flood. It's built by a man whose name means rebel. And in its very construction, its prideful character appears, a character that remains throughout the Bible. It's a city that shakes its fist at God and says, "We don't need you, we don't want you, and we're not going to do it the way you want. We'll do it without you."

From this point on, Babylon has a character; it's a city of pride and rebellion that shakes its fist at God. We know how the chapter concludes. God scatters the nations. He confounds the languages, and every nation of the world today can trace its roots from the city of Babylon. It's the place that spawned all of the problems we see in our lives today. They began at this city.

BABYLON'S EVIL ALLIANCE

Babylon temporarily stepped off the pages of Bible history, but it didn't stay away for long. In fact in Genesis 14, it came on again. In the intervening chapters, God dealt with Abraham, the man of faith. And though Abraham was called by God, he struggled. As you read those chapters, you find Abraham struggling with famine, with family problems, and by the time you get to chapter 14, uniting with foreign invaders. God promised Abraham a land, but others wanted it. In fact, in Genesis 14 for the first time since God has scattered the nations, nations are uniting together. But they're not uniting for good, they're coming back to control the land God had promised to Abraham just two chapters earlier.

Genesis 14 begins: "At this time Amraphel king of Shinar,"—Look who's back on the pages of Bible history. *Shinar,* that country of Babylon, is mentioned for the third time in the book of Genesis. "Arioch king of Ellasar, Kedorlaomer king of Elam and Tidal king of Goiim." Four kings joined together to come and subjugate the land God had promised Abraham.

Of these four leaders, the real leader is the king named Kedorlaomer. How do we know that? Verse 4 says, "For twelve years they had been subject to Kedorlaomer." He's the one who's ruling. In the thirteenth year they rebelled.

Verse 5: "In the fourteenth year, Kedorlaomer and the kings allied with him" attack. So the text goes on and says very clearly, Kedorlaomer is the main king. He's the one pulling these allies together, coming to attack the land. What I love is that God doesn't view history the way we do. God doesn't always put first the one that from our perspective ought to be first.

God doesn't view history the way we do.

As God looks down from heaven, He sees nations coming back together, uniting again. They're coming to threaten the land God had promised Abraham. And so who does God list first in this quartet of troublemakers? Amraphel, king of Shinar. The text then says indeed, Kedorlaomer is the main one, but from God's perspective here's Babylon—Shinar—again causing trouble, and God lists them first.

You know the account. Lot is captured and carried away by these kings. Abraham follows after and, in a miraculous victory won by God, defeats this larger army, rescues Lot, and brings his family back home. On the way back, Abraham stops at a city mentioned for the first time in the Bible.

We pick up the account in verse 18. "Then Melchizedek king of Salem brought out bread and wine. He was priest of God Most High, and he blessed Abram, saying, 'Blessed be Abram by God Most High, Creator of heaven and earth. And blessed be God Most High, who delivered your enemies into your hand.'"

We're introduced to a new king from a new city. His name is Melchizedek, that's derived from *melchi*, "my king," and *zedek*, "righteousness." He's a king and a priest. And he serves the true God, God Most High. He's later pictured in the Bible as a type of Jesus Christ. He is definitely a believing king-priest, and Abraham pays him a tithe recognizing his validity. But that's not the point I want to emphasize.

> **With apologies to Charles Dickens, we could entitle the Bible, *A Tale of Two Cities.***

The point is, notice where he rules. He rules a city named Salem. Now that city is called Salem twice in the Bible, but all of us know it by its longer name that is used far more often in the Bible. The city called Salem here is the city that you and I know

114

by its longer name *Jerusalem.* This is the first time the city of Jerusalem is mentioned in the Bible. And it's interesting that it also takes on its characteristics here. Salem, Jerusalem, is the city where God reaches down to bless the men and women of faith.

From this point on, with apologies to Charles Dickens, we could entitle the Bible, *A Tale of Two Cities.* The first city was Babylon, where humanity shook their fists at God and said, "We don't need you, we don't want you, we'll do it without you." The second city was Salem, Jerusalem, where God reaches down and blesses those who come to Him in faith.

God now zeroes in like a rifle shot on Abraham and his descendants. He traces the patriarchs, their descent into Egypt, the Exodus, their time in the wilderness, their entry into the Promised Land, the period of the judges. "In those days there was no king in Israel; every man did that which was right in his own eyes" (Judges 21:25, KJV). They needed a king.

First, they chose Saul who looked like a king but who didn't have a heart of faith. Then God chose David to be king because he was a man after God's own heart. David united Israel. When the time came to set up a capital where God would rule Israel through David, what city did God choose? Jerusalem. David was followed by Solomon, and now it was time to build God's temple, the place where God's glory would physically dwell among His people. What city was chosen for God's glory to dwell among His people? Jerusalem.

For almost thirteen hundred years Babylon has stepped off the pages of Bible history. And, in fact, it's following the death of Solomon, following the division of the kingdom, following the expulsion of the Northern Kingdom of Israel into captivity that Babylon finally steps back on the pages of Bible history.

BABYLON—THE ENEMY

Turn to Isaiah 39. Three different passages record the same event, but I chose Isaiah for a very specific reason. Let me give you the background. In Isaiah 36–37, the city of Jerusalem was surrounded by the armies of the king of Assyria. Assyria was located in what is today northern Iraq. The Assyrian king had taken most of the cities of Judah and was threatening Jerusalem itself, yet God miraculously intervened and spared Jerusalem.

In chapter 38 at the same time, Hezekiah became ill almost to the point of death. He was going to die, but when he prayed to God, God added fifteen years to his life. Can you imagine the prayer meeting that Wednesday? "Anybody have anything they'd like to praise God for? I see your hand Hezekiah. Yes, what do you have?" "Well, God just spared our city and added fifteen years to my life. I'd like to thank Him for that." Can you imagine how great it was?

Have you ever had a time when God gave you a tremendous answer to prayer? It's one of the most exciting experiences you can have. It's also one of the most vulnerable times you will ever face, because often the mountaintop experiences are followed by the valleys. When we leave that mountaintop of blessing, we're faced with perilous choices and dire temptations. That's true of King Hezekiah.

Following chapters 36, 37, and 38, Hezekiah enters a period of testing and guess who walks back into the pages of Bible history? "At that time, Merodach–Baladan son of Baladan king of Babylon, sent Hezekiah letters and a gift, because he heard of his illness and recovery" (Isa. 39:1). Hezekiah is fawned over by the king of Babylon. In a moment of spiritual weakness, or a lack of

116

trust, he shows the Babylonians all his wealth, and takes the credit for what has happened rather than giving it to God. God sends Isaiah back with another message.

In verse 5, "Isaiah said to Hezekiah, 'Hear the word of the LORD Almighty: The time will surely come when everything in your palace, and all that your fathers have stored up until this day, will be carried off to Babylon. Nothing will be left, says the LORD.'"

Judah's real enemy wasn't Assyria, it was Babylon. One hundred years after Isaiah gave this prophecy, it came true. King Nebuchadnezzar of Babylon marched his army against Jerusalem three times, and after his attacks, Jerusalem was totally destroyed. The king from the line of David was pulled from the throne. There has not been a king from the line of David seated on David's throne since the time of King Nebuchadnezzar. Jesus offered himself as king but the people responded, "Crucify Him! . . . We have no king but Caesar!" (John 19:15).

The glory of God that dwelled in the temple, left, and the temple of Solomon was then destroyed by King Nebuchadnezzar. The people were deported from their land, and King Nebuchadnezzar became the head of gold on Daniel's statue to begin the "times of the Gentiles" that was discussed in the last chapter. Babylon destroyed God's kingdom on earth.

It's as though you had a Super Bowl between the good guys and the bad guys, and as the Super Bowl was played out, the bad guys won. Babylon, the city that spit in the face of God, opposed Jerusalem, the city chosen by God, and in history, Babylon destroyed Jerusalem. Now, if that's all the Bible had to say about Babylon, we could stop here and just be depressed.

But thankfully, God has more to say about this conflict. We're not at the end of the game, we're at half-time. God is saying, "That may be how it played out in history, but let me tell you the rest of the story."

BABYLON WILL BE DESTROYED

The book of Isaiah is like putting your arms around an elephant. It's so huge, it's just too big to get your hands around it. And yet, it's an orderly book.

We're in the book of Isaiah, so go back just a little bit to chapter 13. I love the book of Isaiah. I teach the prophets at Dallas Seminary. Part of my fun in teaching the prophets is that so few people have studied them. The book of Isaiah is like putting your arms around an elephant. It's so huge, it's just too big to get your hands around it. And yet, it's an orderly book.

In chapters 1–12, God says to the kingdom of Judah, "I'm going to judge you for your sin and that judgment's not going to go away until the Messiah comes." And then He looks around at the surrounding nations that are all snickering, and says, "Wait a minute, what are you laughing about? If I'm going to judge my people, what makes you think you're going to get away?"

And then in chapters 13–23, God turns to all the surrounding nations and tells them one by one, "Here's how I'm going to judge you." It's God's grocery list of judgment, if you will. "I've got to judge this nation, judge this nation, pick this one off." God has His list. Who does God put as public enemy number one? Who makes the top of God's list of judgment against the surrounding nations?

Look at Isaiah 13:1. This is the nation that starts the list of judgment against the nations. "An oracle concerning Babylon that Isaiah son of Amoz saw." Babylon was a second-rate, minor, insignificant power in Isaiah's day. Assyria was the big kid on the block. Assyria was the nation that had threatened Judah. Assyria only makes number two on God's list. The first nation is Babylon.

God goes on and describes the destruction against Babylon. I want to look carefully at what He says. We won't read all of it, but let's pick up in verse 4, "Listen, a noise on the mountains, like that of a great multitude! Listen, an uproar among the kingdoms, like nations massing together! The LORD Almighty is mustering an army for war. They come from faraway lands, from the ends of the heavens—the LORD and the weapons of His wrath to destroy the whole country." God announces, "I am bringing nations together to destroy the nation of Babylon. I'm going to wipe out, not only the city of Babylon, but the whole country."

> **God says "I'm going to judge Babylon, and it's going to be on the day of the Lord."**

Now the questions we have to ask are, "What destruction is Isaiah talking about? Is this a destruction in his day? Or was it something future, but something long since passed? Or is he describing something that, from our perspective, is still future?" The answer has to be found by looking carefully at the text.

I notice in verse 6 that Isaiah starts giving a time frame.

"Wail, for the day of the LORD is near; it will come like destruction from the Almighty." Isaiah sets the context of Babylon's destruction in the time he calls the day of the Lord. Now that can be any time God comes to settle accounts, when God intervenes to judge the unrighteous and to rescue the righteous. But does Isaiah have a specific day of the Lord in mind? He picks up this theme again in verse 9, "See, the day of the LORD is coming—a cruel day, with wrath and fierce anger—to make the land desolate and destroy the sinners within it. The stars of heaven and their constellations will not show their light. The rising sun will be darkened and the moon will not give its light. I will punish the world for its evil, the wicked for their sins. I will put an end to the arrogance of the haughty and will humble the pride of the ruthless. I will make humanity scarcer than pure gold, more rare than the gold of Ophir. Therefore I will make the heavens tremble; and the earth will shake from its place at the wrath of the LORD Almighty, the day of His burning anger."

God says, "I'm going to judge Babylon, and it's going to be on the day of the Lord." What day of the Lord do you mean, Isaiah? Look for one where you see the sun, and the moon, and the stars darkened. Look for supernatural signs in the heavens, a time when the moon won't give its light. Look for a time when I'm punishing not just Babylon but, in verse 11, "I will punish the world for its evil, and the wicked for their sins." Look for a time when humanity is going to be "scarcer than pure gold," tremendous loss of human life in this worldwide judgment. Look for a time when the heavens are going to shake and the earth itself is going to be shaken off its foundations.

Now if those images sound familiar, you can find them in Joel 2–3 in his description of the day of the Lord, a day that ends with the coming of Jesus Christ to rule as king over Israel. Or, you may want to go to the book of Revelation, because in Revelation 6–19, these are the very images that are pictured just before the Second Coming of Jesus Christ. In essence, Isaiah says God is going to judge Babylon, not just the city, but the whole country, and it's going to happen in the day of the Lord. You'll see supernatural signs in the heavens, destruction on earth, rapid loss of life, all of this as God comes to judge the world for its evil.

Isaiah goes on to describe an enemy coming in and even mentions the Medes in verse 17, though what he describes was never fulfilled when Cyrus, king of the Medo-Persian Empire attacked Babylon in 539 B.C. Cyrus didn't destroy anyone, he came in peace. But this group is coming, not caring for silver or gold, but to strike down and kill everyone they find.

And then in verse 19, my favorite part of this passage, Isaiah writes, "Babylon, the jewel of kingdoms, the glory of the Babylonian's pride, will be overthrown by God like Sodom and Gomorrah." Now, you have to understand I *love* going to Israel. I tell my classes that it's God's will for them to go to Israel. At the drop of a hat I'll make a trip to Israel, as long as the president doesn't know that I'm gone!

I have thousands of slides from my many trips. I have bored my family to tears with slides. I was taking on average about a thousand slides for every trip I went to Israel. Thankfully, I've cut back considerably since those earlier trips, but I have slides of virtually every location in Israel you have never wanted to see. But there is one place I have never gotten a single good picture of. I don't have one slide of Sodom or Gomorrah. There's a reason for that. When God destroyed Sodom and Gomorrah, He destroyed them suddenly, completely, totally, absolutely, and then covered them with the southern third of the Dead Sea for good measure.

God says, "You'll know when I'm done with Babylon, because when I'm done it's going to be like Sodom and Gomorrah." Now that paints a vivid picture in our minds, but God doesn't leave us there just wondering what He means. He adds on to that. "She will never be inhabited or lived in through all generations" (13:20). Many cities were destroyed in the past, only to be rebuilt. Jerusalem was destroyed, but after seventy years people came back. Because the location didn't change, the water supply didn't change, the roads didn't change, and so cities, though they were destroyed, came back to life.

God says, however, when Babylon's destroyed, it's not going to be dwelt in again from generation to generation. Generations will not live there again. That may imply too much. Let's narrow it some more. "No Arab will pitch his tent there" (verse 20). I love going to Israel because you can still see Bedouin living in tents the way Abraham did nearly four thousand years ago. They pitch their tents in an area, and they'll stay for weeks or months at a time in that area as their flocks graze the surrounding country-side. But eventually when the seasons change, or the grazing land is used up, they'll pack their tents up and move to another area.

God says that when He's done with Babylon, it will look like Sodom and Gomorrah. No one will live there for generations, no one will even pitch a tent there for a short period of time. And then He says that may even imply too much, let's narrow it some more. "No shepherd will rest his flocks there." As the shepherds leave their camp, they keep moving farther and farther from their base. Eventually the flocks are grazing so far from the fold that they are unable to return home before the sun goes down. So the shepherd looks for a cave, a ruined building, a foundation, something where he can bed the flock down for the evening. The next morning they get up and move on. When Babylon's destroyed, God says, you'll know it. It'll look like Sodom and Gomorrah; no one will live there for generations; no one will pitch a tent for a short period of time; no one will even spend a single night. Could God say it any more directly that when Babylon is destroyed it's not going to be there anymore?

> **You'll know when Babylon's destroyed, because its destruction signals the restoration of Israel, not just back to the land as a small scattered group, but as a nation that's ruling over those nations that once held them in captivity.**

BABYLON'S DESTRUCTION WILL BRING ISRAEL'S RESTORATION

Now, beginning in Isaiah 14, God even adds one additional piece to the puzzle. When Babylon's destroyed that will be the time when God restores His people Israel. "The LORD will have compassion on Jacob; once again he will choose Israel and settle them in their own land. Aliens will join them and unite with the house of Jacob. Nations will take them and bring them to their own place. And the house of Israel will possess the nations as menservants and maidservants in the LORD's land. They will make captives of their captors and rule over their oppressors" (14:1–2).

You'll know when Babylon's destroyed, because its

destruction signals the restoration of Israel, not just back to the land as a small scattered group, but as a nation that's ruling over those nations that once held them in captivity.

BABYLON'S FALL IS NOT YET FULFILLED

From the day Isaiah penned those words till today, none of this prophecy has ever been fulfilled. A hundred years after Isaiah wrote these words, Babylon was the greatest power on the face of the earth. Nebuchadnezzar was ruling there. Shortly afterward it fell to Cyrus, king of the Medo-Persian Empire, but it wasn't destroyed, it was made one of the capitals for Medo-Persia. Daniel continued living there. Several hundred years later, Alexander the Great died in the city of Babylon while rebuilding it to make it the capital for the eastern portion of his empire. While writing about events that occurred just before the time of Christ, Josephus stated that there were fifty thousand Jews still living in Babylon.

In Acts 2, on the Day of Pentecost, some of the Jews who had come to Jerusalem for the Day of Pentecost were from Mesopotamia. These are descendants of those who had been taken into captivity in Babylon. The scene closes temporarily as the New Testament ends. But about the year 1000 a Jewish traveler, Benjamin of Tudela traveled to the Near East. He left a written account that was preserved, so we know where he visited. He records having visited Babylon. We know he did because he names another town he visited, Hilla, that is seven miles away. He also records that there were seven thousand Jews still living in Babylon, and he worshipped at the synagogue of Daniel, still on the site.

The veil drops again until the beginning of this century. The German archeologist, Robert Koldewey, excavated Babylon and he records that inside the ancient walls were still three villages. He lived in one as he excavated. Babylon declined in importance, but it has never been destroyed the way God said it would be destroyed: in the day of the Lord, when God's judging the world for its sin, totally wiped out, supernatural signs in the heavens, destroyed like Sodom and Gomorrah so no one will live there for generations, or for a few months, or for a single night. And it will be destroyed when God brings His people back to the land to rule over the nations. Babylon's destruction awaits events that are still future, events associated with the Second Coming of Jesus Christ.

Isaiah has much to say about Babylon. But he wrote when Babylon was an insignificant power. Now look at Jeremiah 50. Jeremiah happens to be my favorite prophet. Those who've studied under me know that while many call him the "Weeping Prophet," I like to call him the "Plagiarizing Prophet," but in a good sense.

The more you know the Old Testament, the more you appreciate Jeremiah because he breathes the Bible. You'll find that he's often quoting from other books of the Old Testament. This man knew the Word of God. In Jeremiah 1–45, the prophet writes to the people of Judah and tells how they're going to be judged.

Then in Jeremiah 46–51, he turns to the surrounding nations and also says that God's going to judge them the way He judged His people. But of the time Jeremiah spends on the surrounding nations, almost half is spent on just one nation, Babylon (chap. 50–51).

"This is the word the LORD spoke through Jeremiah the prophet concerning Babylon and the land of the Babylonians. . . .

A nation from the north will attack her and lay waste her land. No one will live in it; both men and animals will flee away" (Jer. 50:1, 3). Jeremiah says a nation will come to destroy Babylon. Here's a little side point: A nation from the north attacked Jerusalem, and that was Babylon. They attacked from the north, having traveled around the Fertile Crescent. God says, in essence, what you did to my people I'm going to do to you. I'm going to have a nation attack you from the north. As they destroy Babylon, notice something in verses 4–5. "In those days, and at that time," declares the LORD, "the people of Israel and the people of Judah together will go in tears to seek the LORD their God. They will ask the way to Zion and turn their faces toward it. They will come and bind themselves to the LORD in an everlasting covenant that will not be forgotten." When Babylon's destroyed, "In those days, at that time," God's going to bring His people back to the land. Israel and Judah—all the Jews. But He's not just bringing them back physically; He's bringing them back spiritually. They're going to "bind themselves to the LORD in an everlasting covenant."

Later in verse 20, He even says at that time the "search will be made for Israel's guilt, but there will be none, and for the sins of Judah, but none will be found." Israel and Judah are going to be brought back to the land physically, and be united in a spiritual relationship to God.

> **When does Israel come to know God spiritually? When the Messiah returns.**

Now, for those of you who know Bible prophecy, when does the nation of Israel come to know God in a spiritual way? Zechariah says, "They will look on . . . the one they have pierced, and they will mourn for him as one mourns for an only child. . . . On that day a fountain will be opened to . . . the inhabitants of Jerusalem, to cleanse them from sin" (Zech. 12:10; 13:1). When does Israel come to know God spiritually? When the Messiah returns.

Jeremiah says it's those days, it's those times when God will also be destroying this enemy Babylon. Babylon's destruction and Israel's restoration are linked together, not only by Isaiah but by Jeremiah. There's one last point in Jeremiah I want to show you that makes me love this prophet. I want you to know where he was having his "quiet time" that morning. Look at Jeremiah 50:39–40, "'So desert creatures and hyenas will live there, and there the owl will dwell. It will never again be inhabited or lived in from generation to generation. As God overthrew Sodom and Gomorrah along with their neighboring towns, ' declares the LORD, 'so no one will live there; no man will dwell in it.'"

What was Jeremiah reading that morning for his devotions? Isaiah chapter 13! Jeremiah comes along a hundred years after Isaiah and says, "Hey, remember his prophecy of Sodom and Gomorrah?" It hasn't happened yet, but it will. God's still going to destroy Babylon, and when He does He's going to bring His people back to the land and back to their God. They're going to have their sins forgiven at that time.

Jeremiah prophesied when Babylon was at the height of its power. Shortly afterward Babylon was captured by Cyrus. The city wasn't destroyed, but the nation ceased to exist. The Medo-Persian Empire took over, and fifty thousand Jews were allowed to go home at that time. Many of them went back thinking that this must be the beginning of God's promised restoration, the time God had predicted. They went back to the land expecting the Messiah, and found instead trouble, heartache, sorrow, difficulties, and problems. They began wondering what was going on. God called two prophets, Haggai and Zechariah, to encourage the nation. The people were to get busy doing God's work, and they were to watch. God was still working out His program, though it might take longer than they had expected.

I want you to turn next to Zechariah 5. Zechariah had a series of eight night visions in chapters 1–6 of his book. It sounds as though, from our perspective, Zechariah had a pepperoni pizza to eat and then went to bed and just had one dream after another all evening. But these dreams are in an orderly fashion as he relates what God is doing in and through Israel, leading up to the setting up of God's kingdom on earth. The next to the last vision is where I want us to go. "Then the angel who was speaking to me came forward and said to me, 'Look up and see what this is that is appearing.' I asked, 'What is it?' He replied, 'It is a measuring basket.' And he added, 'This is the iniquity of the people throughout the land'" (Zech. 5:5–6). Here's a basket flying toward Zechariah, like a bushel basket only smaller. And as Zechariah looks at it he wonders what it contains. God says it's full of iniquity—wickedness and evil.

The evil contents of this basket are being kept confined with a heavy weighted lid. Notice the next verse. "The cover of lead was raised." So God lifts the lead cover, because He was holding wickedness in. As bad as it was in Zechariah's day, it could have been worse, but God was holding evil in check. As He pulls the lid up, Zechariah looks in and sees a woman.

Now he's not saying women are evil. What he's showing is wickedness personified here as a woman. In fact he says, "This is wickedness" (verse 8). This woman personifying evil is being held captive in the basket. As she evidently tried to get out, Zechariah says, "He pushed her back into the basket and pushed the lead cover down over its mouth." God pushes wickedness back in; He's not letting it get away. The cover's put on so wickedness is held in check.

And then as Zechariah looks, this basket is being carried away. "'Where are they taking the basket?' I asked the angel who was speaking to me. He replied, 'To the country of Babylonia'" (Zech. 5:10–11). Other translations preserve what the Hebrew says: "to the land of Shinar."

Where have we seen Shinar before? Genesis 10–11. That land where evil began. Wickedness is being carried back to Babylonia, to the land of Shinar, "to build a house for it. When it is ready, the basket will be set there in its place" (Zech. 5:11).

> **Prophecies need to be fulfilled, which means Babylon must be in existence again some time in the future.**

The Babylonian Empire had fallen. The Jews were wondering if this was the fulfillment of those prophecies of Isaiah and Jeremiah. And Zechariah comes along and says no, "wickedness is still being held in check." Wickedness is going to be someday taken again to the land of Shinar and set in its place. When things are ready, wickedness will dwell again in that land. Prophecies need to be fulfilled, which means Babylon must be in existence again some time in the future.

We traced Babylon through history and saw two cities: the city that spits in the face of God and the city that God chose. Historically, the city of man, Babylon, destroyed the city of

God, Jerusalem. But God says that's not the end. Before those events ever happened, Isaiah not only predicted Babylon's destruction of Jerusalem, but he also predicted God's destruction of Babylon, in the day of the Lord, when God restores His people. A hundred years later, Babylon did destroy Jerusalem, but God called Jeremiah to say, "Yeah, but that's not the end. Remember Isaiah's prophecy. God's going to destroy Babylon. And in those days, and at that time, He's going to restore His people to the land, forgive them of their sins, and fulfill His promises to them."

Babylon eventually fell to Cyrus. Fifty thousand Jews returned home, and wondered if Babylon's fall to Cyrus was the fulfillment of God's prophecies. And God said, "No, I'm holding wickedness in check, but someday wickedness will dwell again in the land of Shinar. Those prophecies will be fulfilled at their proper time."

BEAUTY ON THE BEAST

And now we go to the book of Revelation. I said at the beginning we'd travel from Genesis to Revelation. We just skipped a few things along the way! As Dr. Pentecost so ably said in the previous chapter, Revelation 6–19 pictures that future seven-year period leading up to the Second Coming of Jesus Christ to set up His kingdom on earth.

In Revelation 11, there was a description of two prophets who were going to be killed by the Antichrist. Verse 8 says, "Their bodies"—these prophets' bodies after they're killed— "will lie in the street of the great city." It's interesting that God calls this city the *great city* and then tells us what it is.

Figuratively, it's called Sodom and Egypt. There was wickedness there. But it's also where the Lord was crucified. Where was Jesus crucified? Jerusalem. Though the city was being profaned by the Antichrist, God still views Jerusalem as a "great city."

Now I want to pick turn to Revelation 16:17, as a prelude. This is the final judgment leading up to the coming of Jesus Christ. "The seventh angel poured out his bowl into the air, and out of the temple came a loud voice from the throne, saying, 'It is done!'" This is it, this is the end of God's program of judgment on the earth. Next event? Jesus Christ is coming back.

"And out of the temple came a loud voice from the throne, saying, 'It is done!' Then there came flashes of lightning, rumblings, peals of thunder and a severe earthquake. No earthquake like it has ever occurred since man has been on earth, so tremendous was the quake" (verse 18).

And then we're told the effects. "The great city was split into three parts" (v. 19). From Revelation 11:8 what city is the great city? Jerusalem. We also know

The best way to understand prophecy, is to take what God said at face value.

from the Old Testament there will be a major earthquake in Jerusalem just prior to the coming of Jesus Christ. The great city is going to be split in three parts.

And then John describes the rest of the cities of the nations. "The cities of the nations collapsed." Ever wonder where Dallas or New York or Washington or London or Paris are in Bible prophecy? Here we are. The great city, Jerusalem, is split in three parts. The rest of the cities of the nations collapse. Then John identifies one additional city.

"God remembered Babylon the Great and gave her the cup filled with the wine of the fury of his wrath" (verse 19). Two cities in the book of Revelation are called great. One is Jerusalem, and the other is Babylon. Now many have taken what follows symbolically, spiritually. They've said this can't be referring to something literally.

I want to say, as I tell my students, take my interpretation with a grain of salt. (Perhaps you need the whole saltshaker on this!) I have come to the conclusion that the best way to understand prophecy, is to take what God said at face value. When God said in the Old Testament that the Messiah would be born in Bethlehem, that didn't make any sense. Bethlehem wasn't that big of a city. How could God know that? When it came time for Jesus to be born, where was He born? In Bethlehem.

> **I ought to take what God says and understand that if God said it, that's probably what He meant, or else He would have said it a different way.**

When God said Jesus would be born of a virgin, it didn't make sense; you have to interpret it differently. When it came time for Jesus to be born, how was He born? Of a virgin.

When God said the Messiah would ride into Jerusalem on a certain day, on a colt, the foal of a donkey, how did Jesus arrive in Jerusalem? On that day, on a colt, the foal of a donkey.

It always seems to me that when God predicts something—even if His words don't seem to make sense at the time—God has them fulfilled just like He said. He just makes the events work.

And so when I come to Bible prophecy, even though it doesn't make sense to me, I ought to take what God says and believe that if God said it, that's probably what He meant, or else He would have said it a different way.

God says in Isaiah and Jeremiah and Zechariah, that the city of Babylon, the nation of Babylon, the country of Babylon, the place where evil started, is going to be around and be judged by God. So I come to the book of Revelation just before the coming of Jesus Christ, and God announces the existence of something called "Babylon the Great." He goes on to say that it's a city. I'm just crazy enough to say, I think He's referring to the city of Babylon. The place where evil began following the Flood is going to be around. Evil is going to return to the scene of the crime at the end times. God is going to finish off what He started in the book of Genesis.

> **Ten percent of the Book of Revelation is spent on the subject of Babylon. If it's that important to God, we ought to try to understand it.**

Now, work through Revelation 17–18 with me. Ten percent of the book of Revelation is spent on the subject of Babylon. If it's that important to God, we ought to try to understand it. What's He talking about in these two chapters? It's interesting that in 17:5, He tells us about a woman riding a beast. She has a name on her forehead. It's a mystery, and the name is Babylon the Great.

In chapter 18, He's describing a commercial powerhouse, but what is it? In 18:2, "With a mighty voice He shouted: 'Fallen, fallen is Babylon the Great.'" Both chapters talk about something named Babylon the Great. Well, what is this Babylon the Great? In chapter 17, after picturing the vision, God interprets it. And in verse 18, God tells us what Babylon is. Notice God's interpretation. "The woman you saw is the great city that rules over the kings of the earth." Whatever else Babylon is, God says it's a city.

What's Babylon the Great in chapter 18? Verse 10 tells us: "The kings of the earth are terrified and they cry out, 'Woe! Woe, O great city, O Babylon, city of power! In one hour your doom has come!'" In both chapters, God is describing a city named Babylon the Great.

Follow with me on this as I try not to numb your minds too much, but that's not all that's the same between these two chapters. In 17:4, God describes the city. "The woman [named Babylon] was dressed in purple and scarlet, and was glittering with gold, precious stones and pearls."

How is Babylon described in chapter 18? In verses 16–17, John writes, "'They . . . cry out: 'Woe! Woe, O great city, dressed in fine linen, purple and scarlet, and glittering with gold, precious stones and pearls.'" It's dressed the same way.

In 17:4 I stopped midway through the verse. The city also is said to hold "a golden cup in her hand, filled with abominable things and the filth of her adulteries." This Babylon holds a cup, and this cup seems to contain wickedness, or evil inside. What about chapter 18? Well, in 18:6 John writes, "Give back to her as she has given; pay her back double for what she has done. Mix her a double portion from her own cup." Both chapters associate Babylon with a cup of wickedness.

In Revelation 17 Bayblon is called Babylon the Great; in 18 it's Babylon the Great. In 17 it's a city; in 18 it's a city. In 17 it's dressed in purple, scarlet, gold, precious stones, and pearls; in 18 it's dressed in purple, scarlet, gold, precious stones, pearls. In 17 it holds a cup; in 18 it holds a cup. The similarities continue. In 17:2 it commits adultery with kings and nations. "With her the kings of the earth committed adultery and the inhabitants of the earth were intoxicated with the wine of her adulteries." In 18:3: "For all the nations have drunk the maddening wine of her adulteries. The kings of the earth committed adultery with her." Both chapters have adulterous relationships with kings and nations. And finally both chapters also have persecution of God's people. In chapter 17:6, "I saw that the woman was drunk with the blood of the saints, the blood of those who bore testimony to Jesus." And in 18:24, "In her was found the blood of the prophets and of the saints, of all who have been killed on the earth."

Now, where am I going? God said in the Old Testament, Babylon was the place where evil began. God says, "I'm going to judge Babylon when I restore my people." We come now to the book of Revelation where God pulls all these threads together. And just before Jesus Christ comes back to earth, God says, "Oh yeah, I've got to tell you what I'm going to do with Babylon. Babylon the Great, that city, is going to be around in the end times. It's going to be a wealthy city, it's going to have influence around the world, it's going to be known for persecuting My people, and I'm going to have it destroyed." I believe God is describing a rebuilt city of Babylon, the city that Saddam Hussein has begun.

BABYLON TODAY: SADDAM'S SURPRISE

In 1990 the world stood up and took notice when Saddam Hussein invaded Kuwait. Most people don't realize however, that same year, Syria invaded Lebanon, in an almost identical type of takeover. Why did most of us not know about Syria's takeover of Lebanon, but were so upset with Iraq's takeover of Kuwait? There's one word that spells the difference between Kuwait and Lebanon. It starts with O, ends with L, has an I in the middle of it.

Why was the world so upset? Because suddenly they realized that one man who had about 12 percent of the world's oil supply could now control about 25 percent of the proven oil reserves of the world. Had he gone into Saudi Arabia, he would have controlled about 50 percent of the proven oil reserves of the world. Oil prices shot up when he first invaded and then went back down when the United States agreed to go in and defend Saudi Arabia. Had the United States been unable or unwilling to protect Saudi Arabia, Saddam Hussein could have taken over and literally in a matter of weeks, controlled a huge portion of the world's oil reserves. This would have given him incredible wealth.

I find it not to be an accident that when I read Revelation 17 and 18, Babylon is pictured as a place that sea captains and merchants are going to. It's a place that controls the world economically with her wealth, that even somehow has a relationship to the Antichrist. The Antichrist is a military power, but this economic power exerts control over him.

God put the oil in the ground, God sets the stage of world history, and I believe when the final events are ready, when the final curtain goes up, Babylon's going to be there. It's going to be there as an economic powerhouse. It's not there yet. Saddam Hussein has not made Babylon all that the Bible says it will be, but Saddam Hussein or someone who follows him could make it that in a matter of weeks. All it would take is controlling the oil wealth and then saying, "I'm going to make that place even greater than I've made it so far. It's going to become my capital." And at that point, Babylon is everything the Bible says it would be.

I also find it's not an accident that Babylon is described as "the mother of prostitutes and of the abominations of the earth." It's the place that gave birth to all the evil of the world. Should that surprise us? Go back to Genesis. Where did the world's evil start following the Flood? Babylon. Though the world doesn't pay much attention to Babylon, God pays great attention. Throughout the Bible this city is mentioned second only to Jerusalem. It's the first city mentioned in Genesis following the Flood, and it goes all the way to the book of Revelation. It's a city that stands against God, and God wants to let the world know He's going to bring evil back to destroy it once and for all before the Second Coming of Jesus Christ. He needs to do that because Isaiah and Jeremiah and Zechariah predicted it. And John says in the book of Revelation it's going to happen.

I want to pull a few more threads together. Keeping your finger at Revelation 17:1, turn to 21:9. We're going to flip back and forth so you've got to have your Bibles ready here.

In 17:1 is the introduction to Babylon's fall. "One of the seven angels who had the seven bowls came and said to me, 'Come and I will show you the punishment of the great prostitute.'" Notice who comes. An angel who had one of these last seven bowls, comes to John to introduce this judgment. Look at chapter 21: "One of the seven angels who had the seven bowls full of the seven last plagues came and said to me, 'Come and I will show you the bride, the wife of the Lamb.'" Only twice in the book of Revelation does one of those seven angels show up; 17:1 is the first, 21:9 is the second.

In 17:1, one of the seven angels says to John, "Come, I want to show you something, John." In 21:9, one of the seven angels who had the seven bowls comes to John and says, "Come, I want to show you something, John." Get the parallels? John is putting this in for a reason. It is not by accident that these passages are parallel. In 17 he says, I want to show you the judgment of a prostitute. In 21 he says, I want to show you a bride. A prostitute and a bride, two women who can't be further apart from God's perspective.

> Only this time the city of pride and rebellion is destroyed forever, and ultimately the Holy City, the New Jerusalem is established for all eternity. God wins. And that shouldn't take any of us by surprise.

In chapter 17:3 John writes, "The angel carried me away in the Spirit into a desert." This could be a place of spiritual desolation or it could be a literal desert, but John is carried away in the Spirit to a desert. And he sees this woman, Babylon, in her gaudy clothing. In 21:10 he writes, "He carried me away in the Spirit to a mountain great and high." "Carried me away in the Spirit to a desert/carried me away in the Spirit to a mountain." In 17 he saw this gaudy prostitute, Babylon.

Who does he see in chapter 21:10–11? He "showed me the Holy City, Jerusalem, coming down out of heaven from God. It shone with the glory of God, and its brilliance was like that of a precious jewel, like a jasper, clear as crystal."

Here is, in the Bible, the end of the *Tale of Two Cities.* Two cities began in Genesis, one shook its fist at God, and said, "We don't need you, we don't want you, and we'll do it without you." One was chosen by God, and He said, "I'll reach down to bless those of you who trust me in faith."

The cities exist through history, and in history, it looks like man's city wins. But God says that's not the end of the story. When the final curtain comes down on God's prophetic revelation, both cities will be there again. Only this time the city of pride and rebellion is destroyed forever, and ultimately the Holy City, the New Jerusalem, is established for all eternity. God wins. And that shouldn't take any of us by surprise.

IS IT WELL WITH YOUR SOUL?

We went from Genesis to Revelation, from here to Iraq and back, but what difference does it make in your life? So what? I think God gives the "so what" in Revelation 22.

I don't know your heart; only God does. You can go to church your whole life, but only God knows your heart. I see smiles; God sees behind the smiles. You either know Jesus Christ as your Savior or you don't. And for those of you who are smiling but who don't know Jesus Christ, God has a very simple answer for you, the "so what." It starts in Revelation 22:17.

"The Spirit"—that is the Holy Spirit, the one prompting

your heart right now—"and the bride"—and He's just identified the bride, the New Jerusalem where all those who trusted in Christ will spend eternity with God. The Holy Spirit and that bride, that eternal city now turn to you and say, "Come! And let him who hears"—those who are next to you, in their heart of hearts if they are believers, want to turn to you and say, "Come! Whoever is thirsty." You're suffering a spiritual barrenness. You've been trying to live a life that you cannot live. You do not have the power of God behind you, because, though you go to church, you have never put your faith in Jesus Christ as your sin-bearer, as the One who died for your sins.

> **What God wants most of all is to embrace you in His arms, to give you your permanent citizenship in the new city of Jerusalem, to give you the free gift of eternal life.**

If that's where you are and you're thirsty, "let him [who's thirsty] come; and whoever wishes, let him take the free gift of the water of life." The first "so what" is for anybody who doesn't know Jesus Christ as his or her Savior. What God wants most of all is to embrace you in His arms, to give you your permanent citizenship in the new city of Jerusalem, to give you the free gift of eternal life.

You can receive that. All you need to do in your heart is pray something like, "Lord, I am a sinner. I know I can't work my way to heaven. I know I'm not good enough. I know Jesus died for my sins, and I believe that His payment was sufficient. I trust what Jesus did for my salvation." If you pray something like that, you will become a citizen of the New Jerusalem.

But what about the rest of you? You've trusted in Jesus

Christ; you've made that eternal decision, and yet you have a heavy heart. Financially, you're struggling. There are personal problems in your life that your smile can't mask. There's hurt, there's pain, there's need. How does knowing about Babylon and God's victory ultimately help you in those difficulties?

I think the answer for that is found in the very last two verses of the book of Revelation. John, after describing all this, finally turns the microphone over to Jesus His final words. "He"—that is, Jesus—"who testifies to these things says,"—and here are the words of Jesus—"'Yes, I am coming soon.'"

Realize if you're struggling, if your heart is heavy, that tonight could be the time Jesus could come back to take you home to be with Him, to wipe away the tears from your eyes, to lift the burden from your heart, to give you the answers to the questions that you don't have the answers for today.

Jesus' response— if you believe what prophecy says, if you look at the world stage and see the events falling together—is a reminder that, "Yes, I am coming soon." And our response in our heart ought to be that of John's, "Amen," or out of the old King James, "Even so, come, Lord Jesus."

My favorite song ever written was a song that I'm sure you know, "It Is Well with My Soul." It was written by Horatio Spafford. You may know the story. Spafford was a believer, a fine man, who had a wife and four children. He lost his law practice in the great Chicago fire and sent his family to Europe while he tried to sift through everything and recover what had been lost. On the way to Europe the ship was struck and sank within sixteen minutes. Word of the tragedy reached him through a simple two-word telegram, "Saved alone." His heart was heavy as he took a train to New York and then boarded a ship to go to be with his wife in Europe. On the way over to Europe, the captain came to his cabin one evening and told him they were very near the spot where the ship went down. Put yourself in his position. You've lost everything financially. Your business is in tatters, but none of that matters because the things most dear to you, your four children, are gone. And the one you want to put your arms around to comfort, and have her comfort you, is missing.

You're alone on the sea, you're near the spot, the memories are flooding back. How do you even get through something like that? We know that Horatio Spafford made it through. We know it for two reasons. One, he wrote one of his sisters, Rachel, a letter, in which he said, "On Thursday last, we passed over the spot where the ship went down in midocean. The water, three miles deep. But I don't think of our dear ones there. They're safe, folded [that is, placed in the fold], dear lambs, and there, before very long, shall we be too. In the meantime, thanks to God, we have an opportunity to serve and praise Him for His love and mercy to us and ours." Then he quotes from the Psalms, "'I will praise Him while I have my being.' May we each one arise, leave all, and follow Him."

Don't you wish you could have that kind of response to adversity? How could Horatio Spafford keep going like that? He sent that word to his sister, and then he jotted down his thoughts into a poem that was put to the music we know, "When peace like a river attendeth my way, when sorrows like sea billows roll; Whatever my lot, Thou hast taught me to say, "It is well, it is well with my soul.'"

I used to sit and admire that man and ask how he could have that kind of peace with God. It was many years later after singing that song, that I noticed the last verse. What kept Horatio Spafford going in difficult times? It was the knowledge of the soon return of Jesus Christ. Listen to the last verse.

"And, Lord, haste the day when the faith shall be sight." He's quoting Scripture related to Jesus' coming back. "The clouds be rolled back as a scroll, the trump shall resound and the Lord shall descend." And then it always used to confuse me, it was like, "Even so, it is well with my soul." You know, Jesus is coming back, and even so it's okay. It took years until I noticed that the "even so" is in quotation marks and is followed by a dash. He is quoting Scripture, but he expects you to know the Scripture and to finish the verse. He's quoting the next to the last verse in the Revelation. "The trump shall resound and the Lord shall descend, 'Even so'—[come Lord Jesus] it is well with my soul."

> God is in control and Jesus is coming back soon.

He knew the separation was temporary, that Jesus was coming, that he'd be united with his children again, that God would explain the reasons, wipe the tears from his eyes. That's why he could face problems and say it was well with his soul. So what does all this mean for us? It means God is in control and Jesus is coming back soon. And as we focus on that, it helps us get through our day-to-day problems in a way that allows us to say, "Amen. Even so, come, Lord Jesus, it is well with my soul." Sing the first and last verses of that song, slowly and prayerfully, as a prayer back to God. When you get to the last verse and you see those words, "even so," add in the final part of the verse that he wants you to supply, "Even so, come, Lord Jesus, it is well with my soul."

When peace like a river attendeth my way,
When sorrows like sea billows roll;
Whatever my lot, Thou hast taught me to say,
"It is well, it is well with my soul."

It is well with my soul.
It is well, it is well with my soul.

And, Lord, haste the day when the faith shall be sight,
The clouds be rolled back as a scroll,
The trump shall resound and the Lord shall descend,
"Even so,"—[come, Lord Jesus] it is well with my soul.

It is well with my soul.
It is well, it is well with my soul.

Father, my prayer tonight is that it would be well with each one's soul. Lord, if there are any who don't know Jesus as their Savior, please prompt them to make that decision now. And for those who do know your Son but who are struggling with pain and anguish and heartache, help them to be comforted and encouraged. Keep them focused on the promise that you could come at any time so that we can all say, "It is well with my soul." We pray in Jesus' name. Amen.

DR. RONALD ALLEN

The Second Coming: What are We Looking For?

DR. RONALD
ALLEN

Professor of Bible Exposition
Dallas Theological Seminary

DR. RONALD ALLEN is Professor of Bible Exposition at Dallas Theological Seminary. The author of 10 books, senior editor of *The New King James Version, Old Testament* and *The Nelson Study Bible,* Allen is a regular contributor to *Worship Leader* and *Moody Magazine.* He and his wife Beverly reside in Dallas.

CHAPTER
SIX

The Second Coming: What Are We Looking For?

The Second Coming: What are we looking for? It seems to me the one answer to that question is going to be very unsettling, but true, nonetheless. What are we looking for? We really don't know. Let me tell you a story.

Years ago in Oregon, I started doing Passover Seders every spring. And when I got into doing those, I thought I'd better keep studying about them, and talk to my good friend, an Orthodox rabbi, about some of the questions that came to me from time to time. I called my dear friend, Rabbi Yona Geller in Portland, Oregon, to make an appointment. I said, "I'd like to take you out to lunch and ask you a few questions." He asked, "You're buying?" I said, "Yes." So he said, "Let's make it a restaurant where I can eat." And so we went to a kosher restaurant, and after we had ordered, he said, "All right, what is it you'd like to know?"

I said, "One thing concerns the wearing of the yarmulke." You've all seen these; Jewish men often wear them, and my rabbi friend always does. I told him, "You know, every time we have a Passover, I ask the men to wear a yarmulke." He replied, "I'd hope so. I'd hate to think of a Passover where men were not wearing one." And I said, "Well, that presents the question. Since it's not in the Bible what does it mean?" He says, "You want I should answer?" And I said, "Yes, that's why I'm paying for lunch." "All right," he said, "I'll tell you." "So, I'm listening," I responded. Then he said, "We don't know." I exclaimed, "You don't know?" I'm thinking about the lunch, but he explained, "We don't really know because it's not in the Bible. It's tradition, and there are a lot of stories that give a general idea, but we don't have real confidence on it." So I asked him to tell me what he did know.

> **The Second Coming: What Are We Looking For? You know, the most honest answer is, we really don't know.**

He began, "What we do know is that wearing the yarmulke is a sign of reverence to God." I had heard that, but I was just wondering about a little more. He continued, "I'll tell you what, I'll tell you five stories, you take the one you like." So he told me five and this is the one I liked.

He said, "Think of the yarmulke as a picture of the palm of the hand of God resting on a man in great blessing and saying to him, 'Little man, you're not such big stuff.'" Isn't that good? I love that. "Little man, you're not such big stuff, but this is a picture of a symbol of God's blessing in your life and you'll wear it in reverence to Me."

I recalled that as I thought about the title for this chapter, "The Second Coming: What Are We Looking For?" You know, the most honest answer is, we really don't know. And what I mean by that is we're talking about heavenly realities, and we are still very much earthly people. Oh, we know a lot, and we're going to get into that in a moment. But before we get into what we know, let's think about what we don't know.

The Second Coming of Jesus is going to be as in the magnificent song by Dottie Rambo sung by Alissa Yearo, "We will behold Him as He is in all of His glory." None of us knows what that will be. Turn for a moment to a familiar verse in 1 Corinthians 13, the apostle Paul's ode to love, to agape, to a portrait of what love truly is. There is a verse at the end of that section that he talks about love. In verse 12 He says, "Now we see in a mirror dimly." You know

> One day I shall see Him in all of His glory. And when I see Him, this will be such a pale image compared to the grand reality.

you can buy a fairly inexpensive mirror today that shows a pretty good representation of what you're seeing, so those words are kind of lost on us today.

I have a mirror like Paul would have used. It is two thousand years old, and there is more than a patina on it. There's a lot of crud and accretion from the ages, but this is a literal, actual, historic mirror from the time of the New Testament. If you could look at the back very closely, you'd see that there are very beautiful etchings of a geometric pattern, suggesting that this was in a Jewish home and not a Roman home, because Jewish people at the time of Jesus and Paul eschewed any design of an animal or plant or a person because of the command of graven images.

This mirror was in a Jewish home at the time of Paul. If we

were to take hand tools and get rid of all this stuff and smooth it out, what we would have is a smooth piece of brass that would give a very barely perceptible, recognizable reflection of the one who's looking in it if the light is right. And Paul says, when I'm thinking about God, and when I'm thinking about heaven, and when I'm thinking about Jesus, everything I know is like looking in this very poor instrument because, you see, I'm still here on earth, and I'm still here in my physical body, and I'm still here in my mortality. But one day, as the song has it, one day I shall see Him in all of His glory. And when I see Him, this will be such a pale image compared to the grand reality.

> **What are we looking for? We don't know because it's beyond anything any of us could ever dream.**

I think of a computer screen where only a few of the pixels are illuminated, but there are enough to get an outline and some assurance of what the picture's about. But now imagine all the pixels coming on a screen as large as an I-Max theater, with billions and billions of pixels, every one of them individually illuminated, precisely colored. What are we looking for? We don't know because it's beyond anything any of us could ever dream. All we know is we'll behold Him, for we'll see Him as He is.

The second way of looking at the topic, "The Second Coming: What Are We Looking For?" is to focus maybe on the what. Isn't there something we do know? And, of course, there's a great deal. We at Dallas Seminary pride ourselves, I hope appropriately, on a wonderful statement of doctrine. It's where all of the professors agree to teach from a certain point of view, not out of coercion, but out of joy. Not out of pressure, but because of conviction. These are things we love.

Let me share with you the paragraph about the Second Coming from our statement. "We believe that the period of Great Tribulation on the earth will be climaxed by the return of the Lord Jesus Christ to the earth as He went, in person, on the clouds of heaven, and with power and great glory to introduce the millennial age; to bind Satan and place him in the abyss; to lift the curse which now rests on the whole Creation; to restore Israel to her own land and to give her the realization of God's Covenant Promises; and to bring the whole world to the knowledge of God."

Did you hear those great things? There's a lot that we don't know, but there are some things we believe the Bible is clear about, and the Second Coming is a part of the hope and faith of the church universal. The so-called Apostle's Creed has within it the words of confident expectation that we believe that He who is present at the right hand of the Father, "from thence he shall come to judge the living and the dead." We believe "in the resurrection of the body." You see, these are things that are not just exotic beliefs of a few Christians in a little place on a backward side of the desert. These are the firm convictions of the people of faith through the ages. And at Dallas Seminary, we've spent time at this, and we've filled in some details that we feel are precious text and precious ideas.

THE GRAND EPIPHANY

So what do we know about the Second Coming? Let's group these ideas on this doctrinal paragraph under three broad categories.

The first has to do with the idea of a grand epiphany. The Second Coming will proceed as the most glorious epiphany of all time.

I'd like you to turn in your Bible to the book of Genesis chapter 12 which describes the first appearance of God that came to our father, Abraham (Verses 7 through 9). Abram, as he then was known, and Sarai, as she was then known (later Abraham and Sarah) had believed God and obeyed God and had left on a journey of destiny that shapes the history of all the succeeding centuries of the people of God. And they came to the Land of Canaan.

> **The Second Coming will proceed as the most glorious epiphany of all time.**

And when they came to Canaan, they did not come just as two old people, hobbling along, leaning on each other with crutches or something else. They came as a part of a vast caravan with thousands and thousands of animals, with hundreds of servants. They came as a movable city, but they were camping in tents. And as they came to the old cities that were already in Canaan, some of which had been there a long, long time, they came to places that had temples aplenty, and every city had altars inside the city walls.

But every place that Abram came, he built an altar outside a city wall, and this was noticed by the people who lived there. This was an unusual event. People would have come out of the cities and from farms, and they would have surrounded this amazing new group of people that was unwilling to worship inside the city in established temples, on founded altars, but instead were building new altars. And they wondered why.

Every place that Abraham went, he built a new altar to the Living God. And when he did so, look at the words that we have in verse 8, "He proceeded from there to the mountain on the east of Bethel, and pitched his tent, with Bethel on the west and Ai on the east; and there he built an altar to the Lord." That's to Yahweh, that's to the God of the Bible, that's to the God and Father of Jesus Christ, and in building that altar, look at what it then says. "He called upon the name of the LORD."

Now an average reader is going to see that and think that means that he prayed to God, and of course he did, but that isn't what this means. More than four hundred years ago when Martin Luther translated the Hebrew verb by the German verb *predigen,* he translated rightly, "Abram preached the name Yahweh wherever he went." He was the evangelist for Living God in the pagan sea of unbelief all around him. So it is no surprise when we read in verse 7, and time after time in the course of his life, we read these astonishing words, "The LORD appeared to him." The Lord was just there, and spoke, and they talked, looking like a man, but there He was. There was a time as Abraham and Sarah prepared dinner for three guests, they entertained angels unaware, and one of them, on that occasion, was the Lord.

I just ask the question how can that be? Since the Father is Spirit, and John says in John 1:18, that no one at any time has ever seen God, is it not possible that when it says "the Lord appeared to him" that this was a revelation of the second member of the Tri-Unity—the Second Person of the Trinity, whom we know as Jesus, the Messiah, the Lord Jesus Christ—and that this is a preincarnate expression of His person, so that He could be seen by a living man with his human eyes and was able to be touched and could engage in conversation? That is, this is an appearance of Jesus before the incarnation—what we call a theophany.

Turn to Exodus chapter 19, where we see not only theophany, but what Claus Westermann, a German scholar from whom I've learned much, says we should call epiphany. He suggests we use the word theophany to describe an appearance of God, where God is all of a sudden there and people talk to Him, and He talks with them and then He walks away or disappears, or He's no longer to be seen. But let's choose to use the word epiphany for what the Bible describes from time to time as the grand descent of God. That's what we have in Exodus 19.

This is one of the most dramatic passages in the narrative of the Torah, the books of Moses. It is one of the most exciting and one of the most chilling of all passages in Hebrew Bible, because this passage is preparation for the giving of God's gift of the Torah to Israel, the giving of the central words of His covenant with them, what we know as the Ten Commandments. Chapter 19 presents a three-day preparation. Sometimes the waiting for something is almost as important as the actual event. On that first day everyone was told to bathe and to wash all of their clothing. This is in a time and in a place where there was a wonder often if there would be enough water to drink, and now they're to use water lavishly in bathing and in washing their clothing.

Men were told they were not to have relations with their wives, not because sexual relations are dirty or unclean, but because they leave you soiled, and they are told, you are to be clean in your person. You're to be clean and focused on what's about to transpire. And there came an evening and the people found it difficult to sleep, all through the night tossing and turning. What will this be like when God comes near?

And then there came the second day, and it was a day of inactivity. They were told, if you have animals that escape from an enclosure, you're not to chase them; you can't follow them. If they go up on the edge of the mountain and you follow them, you may die, because the mountain is now the residence of God, and to transgress His place is to engage in an unlawful act. And they are told on threat of death, "Don't come near." The second night must have been harder than the first. Unable to sleep, they tossed back and forth. What will the next day be like?

The third day came and all heaven broke loose because God was coming down. Can you imagine that—God descending from glory? Now this is picture language, but it's the best language we have. God was coming down, and how did He appear? We don't know, because He surrounded Himself with enveloping darkness. Samuel Terrien, a great scholar, has a happy phrase. He calls it the elusive presence of God, for He is God and we are but men, and what we see of God is beyond anything of this earth. This is not a theophany, an appearance where He looks like us. This is the descending of majesty where He looks like God. And so there is darkness, supernatural darkness, coming down, enveloping the mountain, shadowing it, a darkness that is so heavy you could feel it even as you were at a distance from it.

Then other things began to happen. Lightning flashes, thunder peals, the sense of fire, smoke, and volcanic activity. And of all things, "the sound of the trumpet grew louder and louder." Look at verse 18, "Mount Sinai was all in smoke because the LORD [Yahweh] descended upon it in fire; and its smoke ascended like the smoke of a furnace, and the whole mountain quaked violently." Then the blast of the trumpet sounded long and became louder and louder.

I don't do darkness, I don't do thunder, I don't do lightning, I don't do fire, but I do a trumpet sometimes. The trumpet of the Bible is the *shofar*. That's the trumpet sound that would be louder and louder and louder. And then verse 20, "The LORD came down on Mount Sinai." It's the most dramatic moment of the Bible up to this point. Nothing compares with that.

Exodus 19 scared the people of Israel out of their Birkenstock sandals.

Now, look to Revelation. Chapter 19 describes the return of Jesus Christ to the earth. Not for the church in the Rapture, but to the earth to establish His kingdom, to bind Satan, to destroy the enemies that resist His return, and to establish His glorious kingdom. Look at verse 11. John, the great apostle, looking up to heaven says, "I saw heaven opened; and behold, a white horse, and He who sat upon it is called Faithful and True." Those words go together, that means the truest one of all. "And in righteousness He judges and wages war"—sweet Jesus, the Warrior King—"and His eyes are a flame of fire, and upon His head are many diadems; and He has a name written upon Him which no one knows except Himself. And He is clothed with a robe dipped in blood; and His name is called The Word of God. And the armies of heaven, clothed in fine linen, white and clean, were following Him on white horses. And from His mouth comes a sharp sword, so that with it He may smite the nations; and He will rule them with a rod of iron; and He, treads the winepress of the fierce wrath of God, the Almighty. And on His robe and on His thigh He has a name written, KING OF KINGS AND LORD OF LORDS." Everything that Exodus 19 describes is surpassed by what we read about in Revelation 19. Exodus 19 scared the people of Israel out of their Birkenstock sandals.

In fact, in Exodus 20, after the Ten Commandments, it says in verse 18, "the people perceived the thunder and the lightning flashes and the sound of the trumpet and the mountain smoking; and when the people saw it they trembled and stood at a distance." The point is, these were God's people. These were the redeemed. These were the ones who'd come to faith. These were the people He'd delivered from Egypt and was going to lead, by His great grace, into the Land of Canaan to enjoy Him and His presence until the coming of Messiah. These were His friends, and

These were God's people. These were the redeemed.

they're frightened to death. Can you imagine what the feelings will be of the wicked, when the Son of Man comes in great glory to judge the earth? You see, this is not a private view. The church has always confessed, "from thence He shall come to judge the living and the dead." The Second Coming will proceed as the most glorious epiphany of all time.

Turn to Acts 1. The disciples were with the Lord Jesus in His resurrection body as He was about to ascend to His Father in great glory, and He was speaking with them of coming things. It says in verse 9, "When he had spoken these things, while they beheld, he was taken up; and a cloud received him out of their sight. And while they looked steadfastly toward heaven as he went up, behold, two men stood by them in white apparel;"—angels apparently—"which also said, Ye men of Galilee, why stand ye gazing up into heaven? this same Jesus, which is taken up from you into heaven, shall so come in like manner as you have seen him go into heaven" (Acts 1:9–11, KJV).

It will be in the same manner, the same physical body, now resurrected, now glorious, now transcendent, but still recognizable and wondrous. As Jesus slowly ascended up into the cloud, to the glory of the Father in the highest heaven, one day He'll return. But there are some differences. Even though He comes back in the manner that He leaves, when He returns, all will see Him. Only a few saw Him leave. On Mount Sinai, it was only a few who saw Him descend, only the people of Israel, only the covenant generation.

> As Jesus slowly ascended up into the cloud, to the glory of the Father in the highest heaven, one day he'll return. When He returns, all will see Him. Only a few saw Him leave.

But when He comes to the earth the second time, people the globe around will see Him in the glorious epiphany of His coming. Slow will be the descent, majestic will be the descent, terrifying will be the descent, horrifying will be the descent, unforgettable will be the descent. It is the greatest epiphany in the history of humanity. It is the descent of the Lord in all of His glory.

The Second Coming: What are we looking for? The most glorious epiphany of all time.

THE GREATEST CATACLYSM

The Second Coming: What are we looking for? The greatest cataclysm of world history. The prophets talk about the bad news of the return of God to earth in the person of Jesus by a phrase that's been mentioned a number of times in this book. The phrase is a Hebrew phrase *yom Adonai*. We translate it "the day of the Lord" or "the day of Yahweh." The prophets stumble over each other trying to find adequate language to describe the horror of that day.

Turn to the end of the Old Testament to the little book Zephaniah. Zephaniah shares with Joel and many other prophets of God, a phrase that is the phrase of absolute horror. The Second Coming: What are we looking for? The greatest cataclysm of world history. It's called the great day of the Lord.

> **The Second Coming: What are we looking for? The greatest cataclysm of world history.**

Zephaniah in 1:14–16 writes that the great day of the Lord is near and hastens quickly. The noise of the day of Yahweh is bitter. Mighty men will scream aloud. That is a day of wrath, a day of trouble and distress, devastation and desolation, darkness and gloominess, clouds and thick darkness. I look at all of those pairs of words, and I see a man ransacking a thesaurus, if there were such a thing available, trying to find adequate terms to describe the calamity of the day of the return of Christ to the earth, because when He returns it will be in the worst judgment in the history of the world.

How can that be? How can that be if Genesis 6 to 9 describes the death of all living by the great Flood? How can that be, given the suffering that we've experienced even in our own lifetime, like the recent calamitous flooding in places like Honduras, from typhoons, tsunamis, horrible earthquakes, hurricanes, all of these so-called acts of nature. How can there be something worse than all of those things?

> **In the Second Coming, the judgment will be done, not by water, not by flood, not by fire, not by storm, but by His own hand. Did you hear that?**

I think what makes the Second Coming worse in judgment is that all of those things God did through mediation, that is through Creation, nature gone riot, Creation in upheaval. But in the Second Coming, the judgment will be done, not by water, not by flood, not by fire, not by storm, but by His own hand. Did you hear that?

We're all familiar with the story of the ten plagues. Are we familiar with the wording of Exodus 11? Turn back there where the announcement of the tenth plague is given. The last plague God used to deliver Israel from Egypt, is the most horrendous of the list. There were others that were awful, the turning of the Nile to blood, the darkening of an eclipse that lasted for days and was specific on the Egyptians and not the people of Israel. Some eclipse that was. Cattle disease, boils, gnats, flies, awful things, but none of the plagues is like the tenth. Because in the tenth plague we're told that from the house of pharaoh, to the humblest farmer in the land, and even extending out to the barn, the firstborn of Egypt will die. They will not die, however, as Sunday School lessons have it, by the "Angel of Death," but by the hand of God.

Look at Chapter 11 verse 1: "The LORD [Yahweh] said to Moses, 'One more plague I will bring on Pharaoh.'" He says I will do this. Verse 4, "'Thus says the LORD, "About midnight, I am going out into the midst of Egypt."'" You see what we've done? We've softened this because it's almost intolerable. It's something that we can't stomach. God? No, we'd like it to be done by an angel. God? No, we'd like it to be done by a demon. God? No, we'd like it to be done by a storm or a disease, but God says, "I will do this." And so He did.

Turn to Chapter 12 and look at the summary in verse 29. "It came about at midnight that the LORD struck all the first-born." Not an angel, not seraph, not a messenger, but the Lord. I told you that I do Passover Seders in the spring. The rabbis sometimes got things right, and this they nailed. In the Passover Haggadah, the liturgy for that wonderful service of praise to God for deliverance from Egypt, there is a homily on these words from Chapter 11 where God says, "I will go out into the midst of Egypt." Listen to this. "The Lord, Yahweh, brought us forth from Egypt, not by means of an angel, nor by means of a seraph, nor by means of a messenger, but the Most Holy. Blessed be He in His own glory. As it is said, 'I will pass through the land of Egypt in this night, I will smite every firstborn of the land of Egypt, both man and beast, and on all the gods of Egypt I will execute judgment.' I, I, Yahweh, I will pass through the land of Egypt, I, Myself, and not an angel. I will smite every firstborn, I, Myself, and not a seraph. And on all the gods of Egypt, I will execute judgment, I, Myself, and not a messenger. I, Yahweh, I am He, there is none other." And that's the way it was. When the final act of deliverance was done, it was God who did it. And that was to get His people out of Egypt. And then when they came to the watery mass, and the army was behind them and the Sea of Reeds or the Red Sea was before them, then it was again that God acted in His own person, not by an angel, not by a seraph, not by a messenger, but in His own glory.

Turn to Exodus 15. This psalm, the first psalm in the Bible, is the celebration of the deliverance of Israel from Egypt, and it's celebrated every year by Jewish people all over the world. Jewish people who follow their own Haggadah, know this better than we Christians, because they recite this every single year. When God brought Israel from Egypt, not only was it He, and He alone, who slew the firstborn, but it was He, and He alone, who fought against their enemies and destroyed them. And when the song was sung, verse 3 says, "The LORD is a warrior; the LORD is His name." Yahweh is man of war, Yahweh is His name. And in those words, we are celebrating the fact that it was God, and God alone, who delivered them. *Adonai ish milchamah, Adonai shemo.* Yahweh is a warrior, His name is Warrior God.

That's what we have portrayed about sweet King Jesus in Revelation 19. Jesus, when He comes down is a man of war. Look at the words, verse 11, "He judges and wages war." Look at the words of verse 15, "From His mouth comes a sharp sword." The point is that it is He who will fight directly, personally.

The Second Coming of Jesus: What are we looking for? The greatest calamity in all of human history.

The people of the world don't understand this. They use the word Armageddon which is our word, a Bible word. But they use Armageddon to describe nuclear holocaust, nation against nation. Back in the days of the Soviet Union there was such a threat of the end of the world, we thought, by one nation lobbing missiles against another and though it was thought that was Armageddon, it was not. That would be horrific, it would be world war, but it's not Armageddon. Armageddon is the nations gathered together at the end of the Tribulation period to withstand God the Father putting His son Jesus Christ on the throne of David in Jerusalem. That's what Psalm 2 is about. That's what Psalm 110 is about.

> **Armageddon is the nations gathered together at the end of the Tribulation period to withstand God the Father putting His son Jesus Christ on the throne of David in Jerusalem.**

In Psalm 2, the nations are gathered together against the Lord, and against His Messiah, His anointed. And the One who is heaven laughs in derision as He says, "I set My king on My holy hill, Zion." Do you think the nations can withstand the power of God? That's why there's the greatest cataclysm of all of history. What makes it the worst is it's not water, it's not fire, it's not disease, but it's the Lord Himself who comes to judge.

THE GRANDEST COMFORT

The Second Coming: What are we looking for? Thank you, Lord. The Second Coming will produce the grandest comfort of all eternity.

There'll come a time when all that awful stuff is over, when the wicked who thought they could fight against God would find what a ridiculous position they put themselves in. The

Psalmist David in Psalm 14, viewing their end says, "*sham pachadu pachad.*" "There they will be in excruciating dread" as they see God, whom they've ignored and denied, and with no hope, no time to repent, they face His swift judgment. Finally that's done, finally that's behind, and then we have the rest of these wonderful things from our statement. We have Satan bound. We have the millennial age begun. We have the curse lifted from the earth. Israel's given her land. She realizes all the promises God had given her four thousand years ago, and the clock is still ticking. The whole world, those who are left, those who enter that glorious kingdom of God on earth, are in full knowledge of the Living God. It's the glorious kingdom. It's what we pray whenever we pray in the Lord's Prayer, "Thy will be done on earth as it is in heaven." We're praying for that day.

Again, this is not something weird, something occultish, something bizarre. It's the hope of the Bible, and it should be the hope of all Bible believing Christians. One day, the Lord Jesus will reign in Jerusalem on the throne of David, and His reign will be in tranquility, in shalom, in true peace. But there's a facet to His reign not often commented on, and this is where I'd like to direct our closing thoughts.

It's back to that little book Zephaniah, which is a precis of the prophets as a whole. Not only does Zephaniah describe the awfulness of the coming day of the Lord, but he describes the beauty and comfort and love of the Savior King as perhaps no other prophet does.

Look at 3:14. It's a scene of music. I love music. "Sing, O Daughter Zion" (NIV). When is Zion going to sing? Zion, the people of God, when will they sing? In joy. They'll sing in the coming of the kingdom.

One day in making one of many visits to the synagogue in Oregon where my friend is the principal rabbi, I was struck with something I hadn't noticed before. The service is filled with music. There's a men's choir, there's a quartet, there's a marvelously trained cantor, and there's the singing of the whole congregation. But that particular Shabbat eve, I was arrested by the thought, "There is no instrument." There's no organ, there's no piano, there's no harmonica, there's no cymbal, there's no castanet, there's no drum, there's nothing. In fact the only instrument that is played in an Orthodox Synagogue today, is the shofar on the holiest day of the year, Yom Kippur.

So after the long service, with my students gathered around me and for the interview we'd been promised, I asked Rabbi Geller, "Why is it there are no instruments?" And he smiled and said, "I have a feeling I know how you're going to use this, but I'll tell you anyway." He told us, "This is not true of Reformed Congregations, nor is it true of Conservative. But in the Orthodox Congregations across the world, we do not use musical instruments with our music. For we say as our brethren so long ago, 'We have hung our instruments on the bushes, for how can we sing melodies of praise and happy songs to God in a foreign land.'" But he added, "When Messiah comes, we will take down every instrument known to man, and will we play." Isn't that good? "When Messiah comes, we'll sing like we've never sung and we'll play like we've never played."

I've told churches at every opportunity: you and I who know Messiah has come, in the first Advent, in the life and death and resurrection of Savior Jesus, have more reason than anyone on the planet to love music and to use music in the praise of His name. And as much as we love music today, there

THE ROAD TO ARMAGEDDON

is no music like the music that will be in the kingdom. Because the greatest musician of all is the Savior Jesus.

He's sheathed the sword, He's hung up the shield, He's taken off the battle-spattered garments, He's taken a bath, He's put on the gentler clothes of the shepherd, and He comes now with a smile, and He comes with a song. And look at the words of Zephaniah 3:14. He says, in essence, "Sing, sing with me." I love this. "Sing." "Sing," why? Verse 15: Because Yahweh will have taken away all your judgments. All the awful things are behind, they're all done, there's none to come, they're all behind you, so sing. And they begin to sing. And they sing of joy and freedom, and they sing of sins cancelled and evil done away with, and the fact there's no more reason for weeping or fear. In your midst, *Melekh Yisra'el*, Yahweh, God Himself, in the Person of the Savior King right there among His people. Before, remember the theophany, God would appear to one like Abram or Moses and then He'd be gone. Can you imagine what it will be when He is there permanently in the midst of His people for a thousand years?

Sometimes people ask me, "Do you teach at Dallas Seminary?" "Yes," I answer. "And do you ever actually see Dr. Swindoll?" "Yes," I respond again. "Are you friends?" "Yes." And then I tell them that next week we're having Cynthia and Chuck over for a sleepover. Oh, it's just a joke, but they can't believe it. "You mean you actually see him?" "Yes." Now Chuck Swindoll is an interesting person to know, but can you believe what it'll be like to actually see *Jesus* and hear *Him* sing? In that day, verse 16, it's the end of all fear. In that day, verse 17, Yahweh—it's used here of Jesus—your God, in your midst, and then it's repeated from before to make it emphatic. And then it uses the word that means "heroic one," "the victor, whose battle is done, who saves."

And now there are two things that He does. I just love this. He laughs over His people. In the passion for which He came to die to save us from our sin, He is known as "a man of sorrows, and acquainted with grief" (Isa. 53:3), "who for the joy set before Him, he endured the cross, despising the shame" (Heb. 12:2). And on the other side He laughs, and all of heaven cannot contain the sound of His laughter.

I understand that the founder of Dallas Seminary, Lewis Sperry Chafer used to say that we have it wrong when we read about the sound of heaven that comes when a sinner comes to faith. We think it's the angels who laugh, but he read that

> Jesus, no longer the battler, no longer the heroic fighter, but Jesus with His arms around His people, is quieting them with His love.

word every closely and he says, "No, the angels laugh and they rejoice because of the laughter of God, the laughter of the Father." The laughter of heaven is God's laughter, and in the coming of the kingdom, the laughter of God will be here on earth.

Look at the second thing He does. He'll quiet you in His love. I listened to a program one day when a father called in. His wife had died. They had a two year old daughter. He said, "Every day I pick her up at the end of a long workday at childcare, and I drive her home. I go to the kitchen and prepare dinner, and then I discover when it's time for the food to be served that she's in her room weeping. She just cries every night. What can I do?" And the wise host of this program said, "When you come home, don't rush to the kitchen, but take some time, go to a chair that her mother used to sit on with her. Have your little girl hold a blanket or whatever is her favorite thing. Hold her in your lap and just rock back and forth and comfort her with your love."

I saw that here. Jesus, no longer the battler, no longer the heroic fighter, but Jesus with His arms around His people, is quieting them with His love. And in the end you see in verse 14, He tells the people to sing, because He wants them to sing with Him. He will rejoice over you with singing. Did you know that's in the Bible?

The Second Coming: What are we looking for? Epiphany, catastrophe, and a song.

> **In a word, we are not looking for the Second Coming. We're looking for the Rapture. We're looking for the coming of the Savior for His own, for the church, to catch us up to be with Him forever.**

In a word, we are not looking for the Second Coming. As Dr. Walvoord said in his chapter, we're looking for the Rapture. We're looking for the coming of the Savior for His own, for the church, to catch us up to be with Him forever. But the events of the Second Coming are still real, and they will include all these things and more, far more than we know. But it'll all end in worship and it'll all end in song and seems to me that's how we should end.

The hymn "All Hail the Power of Jesus' Name" has some

wonderful phrases.This is a song that speaks of the reign of King Jesus and it talks about crowning Him. But in this song a lot of things are not answered—questions about the timing of the Rapture, and the revelation of the man of sin and other things. As important as all those things are, there's something far more important for us, and it is that we become the worshipers of the Savior King.

> *All hail the pow'r of Jesus' name! Let angels prostrate fall,*
> *Let angels prostrate fall; Bring forth the royal diadem,*
> *And crown Him, crown Him, crown Him, crown Him,*
> *And crown Him Lord of all.*

> *Ye chosen seed of Israel's race, Ye ransomed from the fall,*
> *Ye ransomed from the fall; Hail Him who saves you by His grace,*
> *And crown Him, crown Him, crown Him, crown Him,*
> *And crown Him, Lord of all.*

> *Let ev'ry kindred, ev'ry tribe, On this terrestrial ball,*
> *On this terrestrial ball, To Him all majesty ascribe,*
> *And crown Him, crown Him, crown Him, crown Him,*
> *And crown Him Lord of all.*

> *Oh, that with yonder sacred throng We at His feet may fall,*
> *We at His feet may fall! We'll join the everlasting song,*
> *And crown Him, crown Him, crown Him, crown Him,*
> *And crown Him Lord of All.*

Let's say Amen.

Our Father, as we sing this song, help it to be truly sung from a heart that is filled both with apprehension and joy. Apprehension for a world of people who are lost, and joy for being among the redeemed. Oh Lord, help us to live as the prophets and the apostles urged us with a blessed hope and with a fervency for those about us. We pray these things in the blessed name of the One whose grand epiphany, horrible judgment, and lovely song are a part of the prophetic future. Beshem Yeshua Ha-mashiach. *In the name of Jesus our Messiah. Amen.*

ENDNOTES

CHAPTER ONE

1. Billy Graham, *World Aflame* (Waco: Tx.: Word Publishing, 1965).
2. Stephen R. Covey, *The 7 Habits of Highly Effective Families* (New York: Golden Books, 1997).

CHAPTER THREE

1. Ed Dobson, *The End* (Grand Rapids: Zondervan, 1997), 14.
2. Excerpts from Alvin and Heidi Toffler, *War and Anti-War* (Boston: Little, Brown & Co., 1993), 247–50, 3.
3. Ibid., 14
4. Dr. Harold Willmington, Harold *Willmington's Guide to the Bible* (Wheaton, Ill.: Tyndale House, 1981), 833.
5. Jamie Peterson, *The Aftermath, Human and Ecological Consequences of Nuclear War* (New York: Pantheon Books, 1993), 16–17.
6. Robert Reich, *The Work of Nations* (New York: Alfred Knopf, 1992), 3.
7. Dweight Pentecost, *Things to Come* (Grand Rapids: Zondervan, 1965), 235.

8. Assembled from Ed Hindson's, *Is the Antichrist Alive and Well?* (Eugene, Or.: Harvest House Publishers, 1998), 122.

9. Ibid.

10. Robert Reich, *The Work of Nations,* 113.

11. Ibid., 119

12. Ibid., 120.

13. Assembled from Ed Hindson's, *Is the Antichrist Alive and Well?* (Eugene, OR.: Harvest House Publishers, 1998), 109.

14. Leon Wood, *The Bible and Future Events* (Grand Rapids: Zondervan Publishing House, 1973), 55.

15. See Sir Robert Anderson, *The Coming Prince* (Grand Rapids: Kregel Publications, 1975, 19th edition); Alva J. McClain, *Daniel's Prophecy of the Seventy Weeks* (Grand Rapids: Zondervan Publishing House, 1940; 17th printing, 1972); Dwight Pentecost, *Things to Come* (Grand Rapids: Zondervan, 1965); Harold Hoehner, *Chronological Aspects of the Life of Christ* (Grand Rapids: Zondervan Publishing House, 1977).

16. Billy Sunday quoted in W. A. Criswell, *Why I Preach the Bible is Literally True* (Nashville: Broadman Press, 1969, 4th printing), 74–75.

SCRIPTURE
INDEX

SUBJECT
INDEX

Subject Index

Nebuchadnezzar, 87, 92, 106, 117, 124

New birth, Rapture and, 40–44

New Europe. *See* European Union

New Testament

future events discussed, 9.
See also Bible

Nicodemus, 41–42

Nimrod, 109, 112

—O/P/Q—

Oil, 136–37

Old Testament

appearance of God, 153–58.
See also Daniel; Isaiah, Jeremiah;
Joel; Zechariah; Zephaniah

One world economy, 93–96

One world government, 40, 88–90

in Tribulation, 55–60

One world religion, 96–100

Palau, Luis, 13, 14

Paul, on Rapture, 30–37

Pentecost, Dr. Dwight, 54–55, 58, 67, 79

Perilous times

Christian lifestyle, 9–21

present day as perilous, 5–9

Persian Empire, 85

Peter, 29

on Day of the Lord, 62

Peterson, Jamie, 50

Phillips Appliances, 58

Plagues of judgment, 71–75

Plain of Judah, 66

Present day

complacency, 4–5

unusual disorders, 5–9.
See also Christian lifestyle

"Prince of the people", 67

Prophecy. *See* Bible, prophecy in

Prophecy Knowledge Handbook, 27

Prophets

Bible prophets. *See* Daniel;
Isaiah, Jeremiah; Joel;
Zechariah; Zephaniah

false prophets, 72–73

Ptolemy, 85

—R—

Rachel, 67

Rambo, Dottie, 151

Rapture, 25–48

Antichrist and, 100–102

as opportunity, 75–77

explained, 33–37

importance of conversion, 40–43

Paul's understanding, 30–33

post–Tribulation view, 63

significance, 43–44

timing, 37–40

Tribulation and, 54

word meaning, 30.
See also Armageddon;
Day of the Lord;
Judgment; Second Coming;
Tribulation

Reich, Robert, 50, 57

Revelation

Second Coming in, 158–60

storms in, 71

Roman Empire, 92

as fourth beast, 87–88

—S—

Sabbath of years of captivity, 83

Salvation

Babylon's substitute, 110–11

how attained, 25–26

Sarai, 154

Satan

as imitator, 90

downfall, 166